THE
PASSOVER
PROPHECIES

THE
PASSOVER PROPHECIES

CHUCK D. PIERCE

CHARISMA HOUSE

Visit the author's website at gloryofzion.org.

Library of Congress Cataloging-in-Publication Data:
An application to register this book for cataloging has been submitted to the Library of Congress.
International Standard Book Number: 978-1-62999-907-4
E-book ISBN: 978-1-62999-908-1

20 21 22 23 24 — 987654321
Printed in the United States of America

Contents

CHAPTER 1
A Modern-Day Passover

WHEN I WAS young, we watched many movies as a family. One of the films that impacted me was *The Wizard of Oz*—a young girl dreaming of a better place than Kansas and finding that all places have issues and there is really "no place like home." However, the movie that impacted me the most (whether biblically accurate in all of its splendor or not) was the spectacular *The Ten Commandments*.

The scene that affected me the most was when God sends the final plague upon the house of Pharaoh and the people of Egypt. God warns the Israelites to mark their doors with the blood of a lamb so that when death passes over each home, the firstborn child would be protected. However, the green death cloud *does* enter the homes of those who have no blood on their doorposts. It is the cinematic depiction of the first Passover, and from that time on, along with Easter it became the most important of holidays for me.

I didn't fully understand the blood, but I did know that if the mark of the blood of a lamb prevented the green death plague from entering a house, we should have it on our door. I also knew that I was the first child and grandchild and understood that the only one to die would be the firstborn.

Each year at Easter my maternal grandfather, a six-foot, four-inch giant in my eyes, would carry a goat or lamb around his neck, which he would butcher and prepare on the grill or in

1

the oven. Therefore, I would go to him and ask him for some blood to put on the door of my room and windows outside. My family thought my imagination was very active and hoped that I would eventually learn how to divide truth and reality. I am still learning by the Spirit to look deep into circumstances to see reality in what I hear and see.

As I grew in the understanding of the Word of God, I began to understand Passover. I came to know Jesus, the true Passover Lamb, and formed a relationship with Him. I came to know His Spirit when I was eighteen. I developed a daily relationship with Yeshua. But I never forgot that green death plague. I formed a watchful eye through the years concerning the evil cloud's movement and activity.

PASSOVER 2020: 5780 IN THE JEWISH CALENDAR

What a shift and season we are in as I write these words: we have just gone through Passover (and Easter) in the year 2020! We have entered a *new era* in history! I will discuss this in the next chapter to better enable us to understand the times we are living in. We recall that when David gathered his men for war at Ziklag, the tribe of Issachar was described as those who understood the times and knew what to do. (See 1 Chronicles 12:32.) In the same sense, this writing should help you with the Issachar anointing that is necessary to maneuver through today's world crisis. At the end I will release a prayer that this anointing will rest on you.

I started receiving revelation in September 2019 that 2020 would be a "true Passover" year. The Jewish New Year, or Rosh Hashanah, is on Tishrei 1. (Tishrei is the Hebrew month that corresponds with September–October on the Gregorian calendar.) This kicks off the great biblical feasts surrounding the fall harvests, which also includes Sukkot (the Feast of Tabernacles). Each year around Rosh Hashanah, my ministry co-laborers and I seek the Lord together to discuss what seems to be developing for the year ahead. We delve deep into the Word of God looking for patterns that relate to the times that are shifting around us. The last week of August 2019 and the first week of September were no different. Much of this time was spent with Dr. Robert Heidler and his wife, Linda. Before I get into the specifics of what God spoke, however, I want to provide a bit of context.

Hebrew was the language that God chose in order to communicate His covenant to mankind. In Genesis 14:13 we find this simple descriptive phrase concerning the father of the faith: "Abram, the Hebrew." The phrase is actually *Abram abar*, "the one who crosses over." Inherent in each person who has aligned his or her faith with the Abrahamic covenant is the ability to cross over. God cut a covenant with Abram and changed his name to Abraham, the father of nations, and then promised that anyone who blessed and aligned with him would be blessed.

Generations later God gave His only begotten Son to mankind. Through the blood of the Lord Jesus Christ of Nazareth, the Redeemer of mankind, we can submit our hearts to be aligned with Him. Then His Spirit, the third person of His Trinity, enters our spirit man and not only aligns us through the Son back to the Father but makes us part of the original Abrahamic covenant. This gives us full access to all the promises associated with that covenant. Therefore, once you are a believer, you too have in your being the *ability* to cross over.

Each year starting at Rosh Hashanah, I always look at the year ahead from a Hebraic perspective since the covenant of my belief system is Hebraic. Hebrew is a whole language. Each word has a parent phrase with numerical value. Each word is filled with sound and with pictorial descriptive quality. The number eighty in Hebrew is represented by the letter *pey*. The letter *pey* is also a pictorial symbol of "mouth," "breath," or "voice."

This new year that we have entered is also the start of a new decade of our decreeing the will of God in the earth. We have entered not only a new decade but a new historical era.

When I began to study the number eighty, represented by *pey,* and the era ahead, the Lord revealed to me a very significant understanding of what was to come. One of the key Hebrew words that begin with the parent phrase *pey* is *Passover*. Most of the world has an understanding of Passover in history; the Hebrew people *crossed over* out of Egypt and started their journey toward the Promised Land.

The Hebrew word for Passover is *pesach*, which means to leap forward and be covered until you cross over into your destiny. Prophetically, when studying this through the Word and meeting with our staff in fall 2019, the Spirit of God revealed to me that Passover 5780 (in the Hebrew calendar) and its corresponding year 2020 (in the Gregorian calendar) would be a very important moment in history. I actually saw that we were entering a decade of Passover or crossing over. I knew we must cross over and keep crossing over until we had fully broken through into the promises for the generations to come.

When reviewing the Hebrew year 5780 from a prophetic perspective in August and early September 2019—and in the context of Passover 2020—I had to stop and say out loud, "Passover includes plague-like conditions." I then heard the Lord speak to me:

> This will be a year that plague-like conditions will
> infiltrate the earth. This Passover will be a modern-
> day Passover like the initial Passover where My people

were redeemed from Egypt. If a remnant in a nation will celebrate My blood and press through after Passover for the next forty days, I will restore, remake, realign, reset, and recalibrate their future! This will be a year that I begin the process of separating and dividing nations that belong to Me.

I want to pause for a moment and clarify a couple of important points. When I first heard the Lord speaking to me (beginning in August 2019) about plague-like conditions that would come in 2020, I felt restrained by God from sharing these things widely or publicly. This is not unusual for those who are called to be intercessory watchmen—those who watch, listen, and act only when the Lord tells them to do so. (We will talk more about the watchman anointing in chapter 6.) Proverbs 15:23 says, "A man has joy by the answer of his mouth, and a word spoken in due season, how good it is!" (NKJV).

On many occasions I have received a prophetic word from God that He constrains me from sharing with a large group of people—sometimes for a short period of time and sometimes for years (or never). In fact, as God unfolded this revelation to me leading up to Rosh Hashanah, I did not share the specifics of it (i.e., the exact phrasing of "plague-like conditions") with even my closest ministry colleagues. Just as with other intercessory leaders and watchmen, sometimes God tells me to keep such things and ponder them in my heart, not unlike Mary when the angel Gabriel told her that the Holy Spirit was going to conceive within her a son. (See Luke 1 and 2.)

BREAKING FREE FROM PHARAOH-LIKE STRUCTURES

I also want to add here that every Passover has economic ramifications. The plague-like conditions that I was foreseeing in late summer 2019 were actually not the most alarming aspect of what God was speaking to me. Rather, my greatest motivation was understanding the *economic ramifications* of these conditions. As I studied and researched, I first looked biblically at the economic models that occurred during Passover throughout the Word of God.

For instance, the favor the Hebrews enjoyed during the lifetime of Joseph ended when he and his brothers passed away. Though the Hebrews continued to grow in strength and number, a new Pharaoh came to power, and with him came a reversal of favor and fortune. The Hebrews were enslaved, and their economic livelihood was stripped away. In fact, their very future as a people was in jeopardy as this unforgiving Pharaoh ordered the Egyptian midwives to kill every newborn male child born to a Hebrew woman. (See Exodus 1.)

Then, in Joshua 5, we see God's people in the land across the Jordan—after forty years in the wilderness they had "crossed over" into the Promised Land. As they began to walk into their destiny, something very significant happened that is supremely relevant for us at this time in history. In Joshua 5 there was a major *shift* in the earth and the spirit realms as God told Joshua to circumcise all the males "born in the wilderness, on the way as they came out of Egypt, [who] had not been circumcised" (Josh. 5:5, NKJV).

In the same way that God needed to prepare the Israelites to cross over and begin to walk into their inheritance, God is circumcising our hearts as a church—stripping us of the things of our past that might block our ability to "pass over" into this new season. In Joshua 5, once the men healed, God told Joshua, "This day I have rolled away the reproach of Egypt from you" (v. 9, NKJV).

Remember, Egypt was a worldly economic power structure that was *not* moving in God's purposes—just the opposite. Today we are dealing with similar Pharaoh-like economic and military power structures in the world. We will especially look closely at China in this regard, which is seeing both a great move of God with its people at this time and a worldly power structure that is maneuvering for control among the world's superpowers.

As I will explain later, my greatest focus since 1986 has been China and how this complex nation will affect the economic structures of the world. Therefore, I knew that Passover 2020 was related in some way to China and how it would manipulate or influence the economic structures of the world.

There is a key principle in Joshua 5 that I want to highlight: After the Israelite men were circumcised and before the people prepared to take the city of Jericho, Joshua 5:10 says the children of Israel "*kept the Passover* on the fourteenth day of the month at twilight on the plains of Jericho" (NKJV, emphasis added).

But it gets better. Once the people of Israel celebrated Passover:

> They ate of the produce of the land on the day after the Passover, unleavened bread and parched grain, on the very same day. Then the manna ceased on the day after they had eaten the produce of the land; and the children of Israel no longer had manna, but they ate the food of the land of Canaan that year.
>
> —JOSHUA 5:11–12, NKJV

Look at this progression:

1. God circumcised them—just as He has been cleansing and circumcising our hearts in this critical season.

2. The "reproach of Egypt" was removed. As we enter into a new Passover season, He will realign

nations—as well as our hearts—so we might *step up* and *step into* a new era that glorifies Him. We will walk out of whatever Egypts were holding us back in the old season and cross over as we seek Him.

3. They celebrated Passover. They began to eat of the land again; after forty years in the "old season" of eating manna and quail, they stepped into a *new season* with new fruit—spiritual, economic, and multiple other types.

Not often, but at times, I look at the meaning of the Gregorian calendar from a Hebraic perspective. In this case, I began to look at the numeric meaning of 2020 in the Gregorian calendar. In Hebrew the number twenty is the letter *kaf,* which means "hand." The original pictograph of the letter *kaf* was a drawing of a hand. When I saw this, I noticed an intersection of revelation between the two calendars. I saw the hand of God moving on the earth and the hands of people stretching in attempt to grab His hand. Even though we have celebrated many Passovers, the Spirit of God began to show me that this would be the year that we would really need to understand it. I knew God's remnant people in nations would be required to reach out, call on Him, and grab His hand by faith to cross into the new era ahead!

HIS SPIRIT SPEAKS

As I was hearing from the Lord last August and September, I questioned, "Passover, plagues, Egypt—Lord, what are You saying?" The Lord again spoke: "Plague-like conditions will hit the earth. February, March, and April will be hellish. I will be watching to see which nations *pass over.*"

On August 27, 2019, I wrote a note in my research on *pey*

(related to speech and freedom) that this modern-day Passover would include an "attempt to take away rights"—in other words, that as people and governments vie for worldly power, there would be a shaking in terms of government authority, the rights of citizens, and what it all means for the church. (We will delve into this more in chapters 5 and 6, particularly in reference to China.)

I saw a death structure gripping nations. However, I also saw the call to celebration. I saw that the nations that would acknowledge and honor His blood would have power to command the death grip to let go beginning at Passover. Death tolls would begin to decrease and would cease increasing.

In addition to what I touched on above, when God was revealing these things to me beginning in late summer 2019, I made many notes in my personal writings that I did not share publicly. For example, in a handwritten note dated August 2, 2019, regarding research I was doing on Passover and deliverance, I wrote the words "modern-day plagues and disease."

Some might ask, "If God was warning you that plague-like conditions were coming, why wouldn't you shout this from the rooftops?" This is a valid question. In this particular case, the answer is simple: God did not give me the release to do so. However, when I *did* feel a release to start sharing this prophetic revelation early in 2020 (more on that later), I moved forward—and this book is part of my assignment to act.

Reader, I leave it to you to divide the Word and ask the Holy Spirit to help you discern accurately whether what I have to share in these pages lines up with biblical prophecy as defined by the apostle Paul: "But one who prophesies speaks to men for edification and exhortation and consolation" (1 Cor. 14:3, NASB).

Finally, in regard to the timing of when revelation is shared (or not shared), a related question can be asked: "Chuck, why did you start sharing about plague-like conditions *after* the pandemic began? Can't anyone then just stand up and say, 'Hey, I prophesied that last fall!'?" Of course, and I understand that logic. However, in my role as a prophetic intercessor (rather than as some sort of doom-and-gloom prophet), declaring this particular word when I received it in late summer 2019 would not have been unto edification, exhortation, and comfort, as Paul says.

PRESS IN AND COUNT THE OMER

Last fall as I continued to press in to the Lord about this coming modern-day "pass over" season related to Passover 2020, I began to study word patterns. As I did, I immediately was reminded that the Israelites *passed over* but still had forty days to *press through* into the promise of their future. Many problems arose during that forty-day period, postponing their promise for forty years. I decreed last September that during the forty-day period following Passover, faith would arise in God's remnant people from nation to nation and no postponement of the promise of God would occur. To be specific, the time period the Lord revealed to me (i.e., the forty-day period following Passover) was between April 16 and May 26, 2020. If you are reading this book during that time period, press in, my friends. If that window has passed, no fear; as you will see in the pages ahead, this Passover season is not just for 2020—it is for the church arising over the next several years.

I then began to see that the real issue would be an economic rearrangement throughout the world. The fifty days from Passover to Pentecost is a time when harvest would flourish, and the people were called to "count the Omer" (the evening tradition of reciting each of the days between Passover and *Shavout* [Pentecost in Hebrew]).

LEARNING TO BATTLE A NEW PLAGUE-LIKE
CONDITION BY PASSOVER 2020

As Passover approaches each year, we again prepare to celebrate "the time of our redemption." In Israel, a Seder is a time when family members and friends come together to sing joyfully and eat delicious food, but it is much more than that. A Seder most importantly is a sacred time to recall the miracles God performed for the Israelites as He delivered them from slavery in Egypt and brought them into the land He promised them.

Soon after our meetings with the Heidlers in September 2019, a new plague condition was encountered in China. "Cases of COVID-19 first emerged in late 2019, when a mysterious illness was reported in Wuhan, China. The cause of the disease was soon confirmed as a new kind of coronavirus, and the infection has since spread to many countries around the world and become a pandemic. On 11 February the World Health Organization announced that the official name would be COVID-19, a shortened version of coronavirus disease 2019. The WHO refers to the specific virus that causes this disease as the COVID-19 virus."[1]

According to the *Washington Post*:

> "Coronavirus" is often prefaced with the word "novel," because that's precisely what it is: a new strain in a family of viruses we've all seen before—and, in some form, had. According to the WHO, coronaviruses are a large family of viruses that range from the common cold to much more serious diseases. These diseases can infect both humans and animals. The strain that began spreading in Wuhan, the capital of China's Hubei province, is related to two other coronaviruses

that have caused major outbreaks in recent years: severe acute respiratory syndrome (SARS) and Middle East respiratory syndrome (MERS).

Symptoms of a coronavirus infection range in severity from respiratory problems to cases of pneumonia, kidney failure and a buildup of fluid in the lungs. COVID-19 spreads more easily than SARS and is similar to other coronaviruses that cause cold-like symptoms, experts have said. It appears to be highly transmissible, and since cases are mild, the disease may be more widespread than current testing numbers suggest.[2]

There have been reports of people transmitting the virus before they show symptoms, but most experts think this is probably not a major driver of new infections. What is concerning, however, is that symptoms can be mild, and the disease can clearly spread before people realize they're sick.[3]

GOD'S PEOPLE CRIED OUT TO THE LORD

A new king arose over Egypt, who did not know Joseph [nor the history of his accomplishments]. He said to his people, "Behold, the people of the sons of Israel are too many and too mighty for us [they greatly outnumber us]. Come, let us deal shrewdly with them, so that they will not multiply and in the event of war, join our enemies, and fight against us and escape from the land." So they set taskmasters over them to oppress them with hard labor. And the sons of Israel built Pithom and Raamses as storage cities for Pharaoh. But the more the Egyptians oppressed them, the more

they multiplied and expanded, so that the Egyptians
dreaded and were exasperated by the Israelites.

—Exodus 1:8–12

As we touched on previously, the Egyptians were frightened
by the growth of Israel. The Jews were becoming too numerous,
too strong. The Egyptians felt like they could easily be overtaken.
However, this was their labor force, and the Jews were too useful
to be permitted to leave the country. What had initially begun
with Ishmael's scoffing of the covenant seed, Isaac (Gen. 21:9), as
well as Abimelech's sons' contending with Isaac (Gen. 26), had
now led to a perfect climate for the rise of anti-Semitism in Egypt.

THE RISE OF ANTI-SEMITISM

Pharaoh's view was that the Jews were too dangerous to keep and
they were too important to lose. When this type of tension—real
or perceived—has occurred in nations throughout history, the
ruling leaders (such as Pharaoh and his court) typically plot to
subjugate or otherwise enslave the group gaining power. Later,
the Romans invaded Judea in the first century BC and made it
one of their provinces in AD 6.

Since time immemorial, the ruling classes of nations have sub-
jugated powerful minority groups. The most heinous example of
anti-Semitism, of course, was in Germany starting in the 1930s.
As many of Germany's Jews thrived economically, they threatened
the German power structure being erected by Hitler. The eventual
eruption of hate manifested itself in the Holocaust and the death
of more than six million Jews.

Nations have to weigh the benefits of using a minority group's
talents against the fear that the very same group's gifts and talents will threaten their nationalism. In the Jews' case, in this initial time of approaching Passover, Pharaoh's treacherous solution

was to deceive the Jews into showing their patriotism by building cities to safeguard the country's wealth. This plan was similar to what had happened during the seven years of drought when Joseph erected administrative cities to take care of the entire region. After the drought, recovery would come quickly and the people of Egypt would prosper again. Joseph had God's heart and was being used for all people.

Pharaoh used this pattern, but with a greed motivation, and had Egypt develop a labor force to symbolize a nationalistic devotion of all toward Egypt. Once Jewish volunteers were mobilized, the plan reversed from the days of Joseph and enslavement of the minority, but prosperous Jews began to emerge.

Pharaoh told his people that the Jews' power and wealth were from Egypt. "They flourished by taking advantage of our hospitality during and after the famine, so now we have every right to take back what's ours!" (See Exodus 1 ff.) This became not only a plan of captivity for the Jews but also an overall economic strategy of control for Egypt. Pharaoh knew that the Jews were too important to the economy to be permitted to emigrate.

BUT GOD HAS A PLAN IN THE MIDST OF CAPTIVITY: NECESSITY OR DRAMA?

The oppressed Jewish population continued to grow. Egypt grew angrier and angrier and therefore devised a plan of population control. *The Egyptians moved from jealousy, greed, anger, fear, and control to hatred.* The plan of labor now shifted to destruction and annihilation. Plagues, a pillar of cloud and fire, and walls of water—God could have moved the Jews from Egypt toward their destiny quietly, but drama was necessary.

> The Egyptians shall know that I am the LORD, when I stretch out My hand on Egypt and bring out the sons

of Israel from their midst.... That you [Israel] may tell
in the hearing of your son, and of your grandson, how
I made a mockery of the Egyptians and how I performed My signs among them, that you may know
that I am the LORD.

—EXODUS 7:5; 10:2, NASB

And again as God was preparing to drown Pharaoh and his
armies in the sea:

Then the Egyptians will know that I am the LORD,
when I am honored through Pharaoh, through his
chariots and his horsemen.

—EXODUS 14:18, NASB

God was determined that Egypt would *know* that "I am the
LORD." Did the parties involved recognize God? The end seemed
inevitable with Egypt closing in behind the fleeing Hebrews and
the sea barring any way forward. God had to demonstrate His
faithfulness as the Red Sea parted, the people crossed, and the
Egyptian pursuers were engulfed and their pursuits terminated.

They got the message—and it was delivered in highly dramatic
fashion. According to Damian Eisner, "The translation of the
word *vaya'aminu* (וַיַּאֲמִינוּ) as 'they believed,' raises another interesting question. Is it enough to 'believe in' the LORD or is something much more significant happening for Israel in verse 31?"[4]

As Hebrew scholar Dr. Richard Friedman points out:

The notion of belief in does not occur in Biblical
Hebrew. In pagan religion, the gods, being observable
forces in nature (e.g., the sun, the sky, the storm wind)
are not a matter of belief but of knowledge. So in the
conception of God in Exodus, God becomes *known*;
God's existence and power are a matter of knowledge,

not belief. When one has seen ten plagues and a sea split and...has a column of cloud and fire visible at all times, one does not ask, "Do you believe in God?" As the term is used in the Hebrew Bible, it means not belief *in* but belief *that*; that is, it means if God says He will do something one can *trust* that He will do it.[5]

Eisner goes on to observe:

This would explain why a more common translation in Jewish sources reads, "they trusted in God," or "they had faith in God." For Israel, the signs and wonders were for the distinct purpose of moving them from *knowledge of* to *faith in*. To "know" God for Israel was a matter of the heart more than the mind. But what about Egypt? All Egypt did come to "know" God in a sense, i.e., knowledge of his reality. But only a few—the mixed multitude who came out of Egypt with Israel—moved from believing *in* God to believing *that* God...is indeed to be feared and trusted to accomplish what he has promised.[6]

The Book of Exodus says:

Thus the LORD saved Israel that day from the hand of the Egyptians, and Israel saw the Egyptians dead on the seashore. When Israel saw the great power which the LORD had used against the Egyptians, the people feared the LORD, and *they believed* in the LORD and in His servant Moses.

—EXODUS 14:30–31, NASB, EMPHASIS ADDED

A FAITH EXPLOSION IS ON THE HORIZON

Just believing is not enough. As we explore the significance of Passover for this current time—a time filled with plagues, wars, and rumors of wars—we also celebrate the past and future redemption during the Passover season. We have moved beyond knowledge into faith, beyond *belief in* God to *belief that* God. We can wholeheartedly trust in God and His servant Yeshua to accomplish *all* that He has promised. Our hope is more than a set of beliefs. Our Seder is more than an exercise of the mind. Rather, it is a declaration of the heart. We base our confidence upon God's unshakable promises, His demonstrated faithfulness, and His guarantee of redemption for all who trust in the One who is coming. As the Master said, "Don't let your hearts be troubled. Trust in God, and trust also in me" (John 14:1, NLT).

May our Passover tables—as well as the redemption of Passover written on the tablets of our hearts—be a source of many coming to know *and* trust in God and His servant Yeshua.

YESHUA PREDICTS THAT PASSOVER WILL BE REPEATED

Passover was the key to freedom in biblical times. Is Passover significant today? From the first Passover until today God meant this to be an ordinance and a celebration from year to year. And especially now, with God's prophetic word regarding a time to "pass over," we take the posture of celebration between the *chronos* of Passover on our calendars to the *kairos* season we are in as a church.

> Take a lamb...for each household....Take care of them until the fourteenth day of the month, when all the members of the community of Israel must slaughter them at twilight. Then...take some of the blood and put it on the sides and tops of the doorframes of the

> houses....That same night they are to eat the meat roasted over the fire, along with bitter herbs, and bread made without yeast....This is how you are to eat it: with your cloak tucked into your belt, your sandals on your feet and your staff in your hand. Eat it in haste; it is the LORD's Passover. On that same night I will pass through Egypt and strike down every firstborn of both people and animals, and I will bring judgment on all the gods of Egypt....The blood will be a sign for you on the houses where you are, and when I see the blood, I will pass over you. No destructive plague will touch you...This is a day you are to commemorate; for the generations to come you shall celebrate it as a festival to the LORD—a lasting ordinance.
>
> —EXODUS 12:3–14, NIV

The initial Passover was not our first, nor will Passover 2020 be our last. As we are encouraged in Matthew:

> Immediately after the tribulation of those days the sun will be darkened, and the moon will not give its light, and the stars will fall from heaven, and the powers of the heavens will be shaken. Then will appear in heaven the sign of the Son of Man, and then *all the tribes of the earth* will mourn, and they will see the Son of Man coming on the clouds of heaven with power and great glory.
>
> —MATTHEW 24:29–30, ESV, EMPHASIS ADDED

In other words, *in* Him—i.e., to know of His existence—will be unquestionable.

MY GOALS FOR THIS BOOK

People of Yeshua, the main reason I am writing—and have been speaking about this decade of a modern-day Passover—is to declare to His church that yes, we are going through a difficult season in the earth, but God will "pass over" His people as we remain covered under the blood of the Lamb!

Before I move into the critical issues that God has laid on my heart, I want to frame the goals He has given to me for this book. This is simply a foretaste; some of these principles may not make sense yet, but they will by the time we finish:

1. The church must understand that we have entered a new decade of war—the *pey* decade, wherein we need to hear God's voice and receive the favor of His hand to discern the critical years ahead.

2. Passover 2020 was prophetically significant, as it propelled us into a new era for the church—an era where we will need to put on the full armor of God (Eph. 6) and remain under the covering of the blood of the Lamb, Yeshua. Positionally in the spirit, we mark the doorways of our homes—just as the Israelites did on that fateful night of the first Passover—and step into our spheres of influence and authority.

3. We must watch, listen, and move only when He tells us to move.

4. The first seven years of this *pey* decade (from late 2019 until late 2026) will involve critical campaigns in the war, giving the church an unprecedented window to move in fullness for the harvest of millions of souls.

5. In both the physical and spiritual realms, the front line of this war will manifest through economic (as well as demonic) power struggles, the realignment of national and geopolitical alliances, and the overall fight for control of world systems (trade, finance, economic influence, power, etc.).

6. The United States is equally at a critical crossroads, and the American church must be ready to let go of the old era—to surrender past glory and the spoils of former wars—and open its hand to receive *new revelation* that is fresh for a new warring season.

7. As we tighten our belts and adjust our spending, the Spirit of God will make us stronger and stronger. As Daniel said, we will learn to do exploits. (See Daniel 11:32.) We will take resources and cause them to multiply in new ways.

My approach to this prophetically rich time in history is one of encouragement. Remember that prophetic revelation must be nurtured. When God speaks to us, we must, like Mary, ponder in our hearts what His Spirit has released. This is a principle that I abide with. This allows wisdom to season and expand the revelation. I have a prophetic team that records, prays over, and ponders all the revelation that we receive, especially preceding Rosh Hashanah each year.

Here is another key in my life: I know I have been given a platform to speak. However, I know who gave me that platform: *God, not man*. Therefore, I must remain under the grace and timing of God to share what the Spirit has released. Just like a person who holds one in confidence, God doesn't want everything He says to be spoken. The Spirit of God gives the unction for timing, which I touched on previously.

Finally, I love the body of Christ and pray for it throughout the world. As you see, I will be discussing the body of Christ in China. The church in China is one of the most incredible in the world. However, the principality that controls the government of that land is one of the most defiant in its opposition to the purposes of the kingdom of God.

Therefore, for me to prophesy, I must divide asunder my emotions and allow love to rule before I speak. In all instances, *love* produces *faith*. Discernment must be held until love can be developed. *We prophesy according to our faith!*

CHAPTER 2
A Modern-Day Plague

ACK IN 2007 I wrote the following in *God's Unfolding Battle Plan*:

> The fear of pandemic viruses and biological warfare will continue to increase in the world, but God's people will have confidence that He can cleanse and filter our blood in new ways. I believe that God will have people who create filtering processes that can cleanse a person's blood in less than an hour. Things such as the SARS virus will not create fear worldwide. Not only will God create natural ways to cleanse blood, but He will supernaturally set a blood barrier for His people so that these viruses cannot enter them.[1]

When I first wrote those words, I really never thought the crisis of COVID-19 that is raging today would affect the world like we see happening. This virus, however, will become a model for what is ahead for mankind. Here are some key worldwide statistics of deaths that have occurred in the first several months of this year:

Worldwide deaths from January 1 through May 10, 2020:

- 173,899—Deaths by seasonal flu
- 282,733—Deaths by coronavirus
- 350,444—Deaths by malaria

- 383,122—Deaths by suicides
- 482,284—Deaths by traffic fatalities
- 893,580—Deaths by alcohol
- 1,786,037—Deaths by smoking
- 2,934,288—Deaths by cancer
- 15,189,908—Deaths by abortion[2]

IS COVID-19 A PLAGUE OR MEDIA PANDEMIC?

At first glance, you might wonder why such precautions needed to be taken worldwide to attempt to stop the spread of this deadly morphing virus. Why is COVID-19 worse than common flu? We saw results of this virus being more contagious and more deadly for the elderly than other flus. In America, the city of New Orleans had a high per capita occurrence because of pre-existing conditions like hypertension, obesity, and diabetes. This virus also had the potential to overwhelm a health system that needed a full makeover.

In Corinth, Texas, at Global Spheres Center we record all prophecies and revelation that are brought forth during our prayer, intercession, worship, and corporate gatherings. As in the early church, we have learned the importance of present truth and interpretation of times. On January 13, 2020, I prophesied the following:

> There is a truth that I will uncover coming out of China that has never been seen before. Get ready—for I am going to oil the church in China. A new anointing will fall on that church, and because of that, the truth that is not seen will begin to be uncovered. Get ready—the oil of My anointing is beginning to squirt on My church that has had to pull back and remain hidden

over these last several years. Because of the anointing, the sheet of deception in China will be lifted.

My breath is beginning to blow and cause an awakening in the nations. Submit as I draw you near. Resist the enemy and he must start backing away. Territories will now start awakening to the enemy's plan. This is the beginning of an awakening conquest throughout the earth…a remnant will arise with the sound of awakening. This will snap in place new borders and boundaries. What has been contending for My people will not triumph, for I will order new borders for their lives. People are being repositioned. They're letting go of places where they have been and are being rebordered for a new portion.

Structures are beginning to say, "We have to reform." The health structure in America will start reforming from heaven because the spirit of penetration is coming to kill and rearrange. I will begin a healing move that will bypass the health system. Decree to nations, states, or wherever you are that the borders around you are reawakening and coming alive!

Scientifically, *plague* refers to bubonic plague, which is bacterial. The term is used linguistically to refer to a widespread devastation of any kind. Biblically, the word *plague* means a blow or affliction. Its root word means "to lay the hand upon." That is why this year becomes important in the *pey* (hand) decade in which we are living. *Pandemic* is a term that refers to the geographic spread of a new virus across the globe. This takes place because as new strains emerge, there is little to no preexisting immunity to halt the spread.

A question often raised about the COVID-19 pandemic is whether this disease is a lot like the flu. Some of the symptoms of

COVID-19 resemble flu—especially fever and cough. But this virus is worse for the destruction it may cause, not only in human lives but also to our society. And COVID-19 hasn't been around a year—or even half a year at the time of this writing. According to a March 18, 2020, article that ran in Vox.com:

> Before January [2020], this virus was not known to science....And while there is still a lot of uncertainty over this virus, and how it will play out, from what we know so far, this is a threat to take extremely seriously....Sober-minded epidemiologists say that 20 to 60 percent of the world's adult population could end up catching this virus....It's possible that Covid-19 will become endemic—meaning it will be a disease that regularly attacks humans and will not go away until there's a treatment or a vaccine.[3]

GOD'S WAR TO BRING FORTH LIFE

God has given us a wonderful cycle of life designed to release ever-increasing blessing into our lives. The first key appointed time in this yearly cycle is the Feast of Passover. (God's "appointed times" are also called "biblical feasts" or "the festivals of the Lord.")

To put these key times in perspective, it's helpful to understand what the Bible means when it talks about a feast or festival. In *A Time to Prosper*, Robert Heidler and I share about God's heart for the feasts:

> In the Old Testament several Hebrew words are used to designate God's appointed times. One word used is *mo'ed*, which simply means "an appointed time." It designated an occasion fixed by divine appointment to meet together for fellowship with God and worship. Another Hebrew word used for one of these special

days is *hag,* which is taken from the verb "to dance" and means, "an occasion of joy or gladness." A third Hebrew word used of a God-appointed time is *hagag.* This word has a variety of meanings:

- To celebrate a special day.

- Rejoicing!

- The festive attitudes and actions of celebrating a feast.

- Wild and unrestrained actions, like the behavior of a drunken person. (It's interesting to note that on Pentecost, the apostles so overflowed with the Spirit that their actions appeared to be those of a drunken people.)

- Festive dancing and celebrations, as of a victory over enemies in battle.

From looking at these words, we can begin to get a sense of what holding a festival to the Lord, such as Passover or Tabernacles, was meant to be: a time of rejoicing and celebration with the kind of unrestrained joy you would experience when you were victorious in a battle!

This gives us real insight into the heart of God! God could have designed His appointed times to be times of sorrow. He could have made them times of severe fasting and repentance. That's how some view God! Greek Paganism taught that suffering makes a person holy. This belief, called *"asceticism,"* still affects much of the Church today. Many Christians assume God wants them to show their devotion to Him by being *miserable.* But that's not in the Bible! There *are* times for fasting and self-denial, but *most* of God's appointed times are times of *feasting*! God wants us to know that He desires for His children to *enjoy* Him and experience His *goodness*![4]

THE PASSOVER TIME

Most Christians today know very little about Passover. We don't know what it is or how to celebrate it. If you are not familiar with Passover, here's a one-sentence summary:

> Passover is a celebration of redemption and deliverance by the blood of the Lamb.

For the Jews, Passover was a celebration of God's power in setting them free from slavery in Egypt. They had been in bondage, under bitter oppression, but they cried out to God and He delivered them *through Passover.*

Christians also have a deliverance to celebrate! We have also been in bondage, under the oppression of a cruel enemy: Satan. Passover is a vivid picture of how God delivered *us.* To understand Passover, it is good to ask, "What was 'passed over' at Passover?" The answer is the *Israelites* were passed over. The time had come for God's judgment to fall. It would have fallen on everyone, but God gave the Israelites a way of escape. The key to their rescue was not in an army. It was not in some great, heroic deed but in a pure, spotless lamb. When the blood of the lamb was placed on the doorposts, God accepted the death of that lamb in place of Israel's firstborn. The angel of death *passed over* them. Many things happened at Passover.

By the blood of that lamb, Israel was *redeemed*! The judgment of God was turned away from them! The gods of Egypt were judged, their power broken! Israel was released from oppression and bondage! They were set free to enter God's promise!

PLAGUES FROM THE FIRST PASSOVER UNTIL NOW

Let's look further at the ten plagues of the first Passover and what was really going on with these plagues. These were never about the plague per se. These plagues were about forcing a new freedom and movement in the earth. In *Time to Defeat the Devil*, I share about this in more detail.[5]

PLAGUE ONE—THE NILE RIVER TURNS TO BLOOD

In ancient Egypt the Nile River was looked at as the source of life. It provided both food and water for the people. Each year it would flood and leave a layer of fertile silt in which their next year's crops would flourish. Two gods were closely associated with the Nile. One was the god Hapi, and the other was the god Khenmu or Khnum. Hapi was worshipped as the god of the Nile. He was thought to be responsible for the fish, birds, and fertile soil that the Nile River brought to the people of Egypt. Without the Nile River the people would have died, so Hapi was sometimes revered more than Ra, the sun god.

Along with Hapi, Khnum was also worshipped as a god of the Nile. He was called the potter god. He was believed to be the one who formed human bodies from the silt of the Nile on his potter's wheel. These two gods were viewed as the source of life. Khnum formed your body, and Hapi provided the food and water necessary for life to be sustained, so these two gods were, to the Egyptians, the source and sustainer of life. While we would never say that we believe we were created by a potter like Khnum or that our lives are sustained by a god like Hapi, we sometimes look at material things or even the forces of nature the way the Egyptians viewed these gods.

PLAGUE TWO—FROGS

The second plague God sent on Egypt was closely related to the first, since the frogs came out of the Nile. It wasn't unusual for frogs to come up from the Nile. Each year after the Nile flooded, frogs would begin to appear. They were looked at as a symbol of fertility and of new life springing forth from the Nile River.

The goddess associated with frogs was Heket. She was a goddess of childbirth, creation, and grain germination. As a water goddess, she was also a goddess of fertility and childbirth, particularly associated with the later stages of labor. She was thought to be the wife of Khnum, the god who created men on his potter's wheel. The Egyptians believed she gave a child the breath of life before it was placed in the mother's womb.

If Hapi and Khnum were the source and sustainers of life, then Heket was the goddess who ensured a future generation. Midwives worshipped Heket as the one who would help them to give a safe birth to children. It's interesting that the Hebrew midwives were known to *fear God* rather than Heket and would not kill the male children born to the Israelite women, in spite of Pharaoh's edict.

PLAGUE THREE—STINGING GNATS

In Exodus 8:16 God told Moses to have Aaron strike the earth, and the dust would become stinging gnats that would cover the land of Egypt. This was a direct confrontation with the Egyptian god Geb, who was believed to be the god of the earth.

Some translations say this was a plague of lice, which would be bad enough, but a better translation is probably "stinging gnats." These were tiny gnats, almost invisible, that would inflict a painful sting. And they were everywhere! Their stings some-times became infected, producing a painful sore. Suddenly the Egyptians' faith in Geb was shaken. Instead of the earth bringing forth food to nourish them, it was bringing forth stinging gnats. And Geb, the god of the earth, had no power to stop them. Overcoming Geb means to overcome the fear of death. Geb was worshipped because it was believed he had the power to hold you in the grave or release you into the afterlife. But if Geb lacked power over something as small as a gnat, then how could you trust him with your future after death?

PLAGUE FOUR—FLIES (OR SCARAB BEETLES)

After the plague of stinging gnats, the Lord threatened to send a plague of flies. Some translations say it was scarab beetles—also called dung beetles—but a more likely translation is "flies." Whichever insect it was, the Egyptians felt they didn't need to worry much about it, because one of their most powerful gods was in control of insects. His name was Khepri, and both beetles and flies were supposedly under his control. He was thought to be such a powerful god that he even controlled creation and person-ally moved the sun across the sky each day.

PLAGUE FIVE—LIVESTOCK

Hathor, the Egyptian cow goddess, was next in line for humili-ation at the hands of God's wrath. She was the suckler of the king and the goddess of love, fertility, and women. She was also said to cleanse the land of unbelievers. This plague was a judgment from God and a direct insult to the religious hierarchy, as calves, cows, and bulls were all worshipped and considered by the Egyptians.

PLAGUE SIX—BOILS

When the Lord dealt with the Egyptians in the sixth plague, the system of healing they used was affected. In the plague of boils, God directly challenged the power of the Egyptian gods to heal. Egypt is often thought of as having been medically advanced for an ancient civilization. The reason for this is that the Egyptians were riddled with every kind of disease and infirmity. Healing and cures were very important parts of their lives. For them, healing was not a matter of medicine but of magic.

Different ailments, diseases, or injuries were attributed to different gods or goddesses who could either cause or prevent infirmity. There was a goddess associated with snake or scorpion bites. Another goddess could send or cure disease. Still another god was responsible for wounds or injuries. Each kind of ailment had a corresponding ritual, potion, and amulet to appease the god or goddess who could bring about healing. Physicians guarded the secrets and mysteries of healing. For all of this, the ancient Egyptians were not a healthy people.

One of their rituals for healing was particularly gruesome. It's said that they would offer a human sacrifice, burning the victim alive on a high altar, and then scatter the ashes into the air. It was believed that with every scattered ash the blessing of healing would descend upon the people. When Moses took a handful of soot and tossed it into the air, it was a direct confrontation of this belief. It caused boils to break out that none of the Egyptian physicians or magicians could heal. The gods of Egypt were shown to be powerless.

PLAGUE SEVEN—HAIL

In Egypt the goddess associated with the sky was Nut. She provided a barrier separating the forces of chaos from the ordered cosmos in this world. She was the wife of Geb, the earth god, and was looked at as the protector of the earth. Nut was especially noted as the goddess of the night sky, with the stars and constellations predicting the future. Nut was one of the most important goddesses. People believed that their protection from the destructive forces of nature was dependent upon serving her. When hail came from the sky to destroy crops, animals, and people, the power of Nut to protect was shown to be ineffective.

PLAGUE EIGHT—LOCUSTS

In the plague of locusts, God was overcoming a host of Egyptian gods. Shu was the god who controlled the winds, so God sent the locusts in on the east wind. Nephri was the goddess who guarded the grain, and Renenutet was the goddess who guarded the harvest, so God sent locusts to devour the grain and wipe out the harvest. Geb was the god of the earth, so God sent locusts to strip the earth of all vegetation. Heset was the god of plenty, so God sent the locusts to remove the Egyptians' prosperity. These gods were all counted on to produce and secure a good harvest for prosperity.

PLAGUE NINE—DARKNESS

The ninth plague God sent on Egypt was darkness. This was no ordinary darkness. Exodus 10:21 (NASB) says that this darkness could even be "felt." Exodus 10:22 (NASB) says that it was "thick darkness"—a total absence of light. The highest god of Egypt was Ra, the sun god, the bringer of light. An adversary to Ra was the god Apep, who ruled the darkness. What God sent on Egypt was actually a confrontation with both Ra and Apep. By sending a darkness that was deeper and longer than any they had ever known, the Lord showed His power over Ra. He showed that He could prevent the sun from shining on the Egyptians. But by allowing the sun to shine in Goshen, where the Hebrews lived,

He showed His power over the Egyptian god of darkness. The Lord could bring light wherever He chose.

PLAGUE TEN—DEATH OF THE FIRSTBORN

The power of the blood frees us! Through plague after plague, God confronted the gods of Egypt. Yet Pharaoh still would not let the people go. One of the highest gods of Egypt was Pharaoh himself. He was viewed as a god and not only was the ultimate authority in the land but also demanded worship. He was the one who could decide to let the people go or force them to remain in Egypt. So this plague was directed at the thing most important to Pharaoh.

This plague seems terribly harsh, but we need to see that it was really Egypt's own sin revisited upon them. But there was an offer of grace! No Egyptian had to see his or her firstborn die. God provided a way of escape for anyone who would receive it. But Pharaoh was so sure of his own power that he refused to give in. Pharaoh's confidence was in his own strength and in the protection of Isis, the goddess who guarded children.

God doesn't want us to fall into Pharaoh's trap! He doesn't want us to trust in our own strength or any other power. God has a provision of grace for all who will receive it. In Egypt, God allowed a lamb to die in place of the firstborn. Many centuries later, this is still God's provision. He gave His firstborn Son, the Lamb of God, to die—not just for the firstborn but for all mankind.

Our victory over death does not come by the strength of our will or from any other supernatural power. It comes from the power of the blood of Jesus. First Corinthians 15:26 says that the last enemy we overcome is death. This was true for Israel coming out of Egypt, and it is true for us today. How we face that enemy and overcome depends on what we are counting on for our victory. Thank God that His Son died in your place.

Passover was commanded by God for the Jews in the Old Testament to teach them the importance of redemption by the blood. But it was also observed by Christians in the New Testament to remember God's redeeming work. The Bible tells us it is to be a *permanent* ordinance—a celebration for all time. Many Christians don't realize that Passover is just as much a New Testament feast as an Old Testament feast! It is all through the New Testament. Jesus and the apostles all celebrated Passover. The original Lord's Supper was a Passover meal. The apostles taught the Gentile churches to celebrate Passover. In 1 Corinthians, Paul wrote to a predominantly Gentile church and said, "For indeed Christ, our Passover, was sacrificed for us. Therefore let us keep the feast" (1 Cor. 5:7–8, NKJV). For hundreds of years Passover was the most important yearly celebration in the early church!

WHAT MAKES PASSOVER SO IMPORTANT?

Derek Prince once said that the most powerful faith declaration for deliverance is this: "I am redeemed by the blood of the Lamb out of the hand of the enemy!" He said if you can make that declaration in faith and keep on making it, something will happen. You will be delivered from the power of the enemy. That's really the message of Passover. The Feast of Passover is a faith declaration that we are redeemed by the blood of the Lamb. It does something in us when we celebrate Passover. When we come together to remember God's great works of redemption and declare the power of redemption in our lives, it *always* does something!

SATAN HATES PASSOVER!

Satan knows when you lay hold of the blood of the Lamb by faith, his hold on you is broken! That's why Satan would always rather give you an Easter bunny than a Passover lamb. The power is in the blood! Down through history, Satan has worked diligently to steal Passover away. There's always a battle for Passover. We see it in church history. In the fourth century when the emperor Constantine tried to merge Christianity and paganism, it sounded like a good deal to many. He legalized Christianity so people could go to church without having to fear being thrown to the lions. Constantine didn't mind Christians having a celebration of Jesus' resurrection. But he did have an issue with Passover. He demanded that Christians *not* celebrate Jesus' resurrection at the time of Passover. At the Council of Nicaea (AD 325) he declared, "This irregularity [observing Passover] MUST be corrected!"

At the council of Nicaea, Constantine *outlawed Passover* and directed that Christ's death and resurrection be celebrated on "the Sunday following the first full moon after the vernal equinox," a time associated with the spring festival of the pagan fertility goddess Ishtar, also known as Eastre! (That's why in the church today we celebrate the resurrection at Easter instead of Passover.) Constantine's goal was to remove Jesus from the context of Passover.

THE BATTLE CONTINUES

Many in the church resisted Constantine's edicts, so for many centuries after Constantine the battle for Passover continued. In the sixth century, for example, Emperor Justinian sent the Roman armies throughout the empire to enforce the prohibition on Passover. In his attempt to wipe out the "heresy" of Passover, thousands of men, women, and children were brutally murdered. Entire cities were massacred for refusing to stop celebrating Passover. Pressured by the government, the Roman church joined in the attempts to stamp out Passover. Notice some of the decrees passed against Passover by various church councils:

- The Council of Antioch (AD 345)—"If any bishop, presbyter or deacon will dare, after this decree, to celebrate Passover, the council judges them to be anathema from the church. This council not only deposes them from ministry, but also any others who dare to communicate with them." (The word *anathema* means "cursed." The church actually pronounced a curse on Christians who would celebrate Passover.)

- The Council of Laodicea (AD 365)—"It is not permitted to receive festivals which are by Jews."

- The Council of Agde, France (AD 506)—"Christians must not take part in Jewish festivals."

- The Council of Toledo X (seventh century)—"Easter must be celebrated at the time set by the decree of Nicaea."

THE BATTLE FOR PASSOVER IS SEEN CLEARLY IN CHURCH HISTORY

That battle against Passover is nothing new. We see the same thing in the Bible: Satan *always* tries to steal away Passover because he knows the celebration of the blood releases power. Look what happened in Hezekiah's day.

Hezekiah did what was right in the eyes of the Lord. He repaired and cleansed the temple, tore down the false altars, and restored the sacrifices and Davidic praise. Then Hezekiah sent word to all Israel and Judah, inviting them to come to celebrate Passover. Couriers went throughout Israel and Judah saying, "People of Israel, return to the Lord." The hand of God was on the people to give them unity of mind to carry out what the king had ordered. A very large crowd of people assembled in Jerusalem to celebrate the feast. They slaughtered the Passover lamb and celebrated the feast for seven days with great rejoicing while the Levites sang to the Lord every day, accompanied by instruments of praise. The whole assembly then agreed to celebrate the festival seven more days, so for another seven days they celebrated joyfully. "There was great joy in Jerusalem, for since the time of Solomon the son of David, king of Israel, there had been nothing like this in Jerusalem. Then the priests, the Levites, arose and blessed the people, and their voice was heard; and their prayer came up to His holy dwelling place, to heaven" (2 Chron. 30:26–27, NKJV).

The same thing was happening in Josiah's day, as we see in 2 Kings 22–23. Josiah did what was right in the eyes of the Lord. In the eighteenth year of his reign, while repairing the temple, the Israelites found the Torah scroll in the temple. When the king heard the words of the Torah scroll, he tore his robes. He went up to the temple with all the people. He read in their hearing all the words of the covenant. Then all the people pledged themselves to the covenant. The king ordered them to remove from the temple all the idols made for Baal and Asherah and all the starry hosts. He tore down the quarters of the male prostitutes, which were in the temple. The king gave this order to all the people: "Keep the Passover to the LORD your God, as it is written in this Book of the Covenant" (2 Kings 23:21, NKJV). In the eighteenth year of King Josiah, this Passover was celebrated to the Lord in Jerusalem. Not since the days of the judges who led Israel, nor throughout the days of the kings of Israel and the kings of Judah, had such a Passover been observed.

WE SEE A BIBLICAL PATTERN

In both of these accounts, God's people had drifted far from the Lord and turned to idolatry, and the blessing of God was lost.

They turned back to God and sought Him, and the first thing God did was restore Passover. As they turned from pagan idols and celebrated Passover, they were restored to God and experienced great joy and blessing. That's an interesting pattern. Over and over again in the Bible, we discover that Passover had been *lost*! During the Old Testament era, and even among the Jews, generations lived and died without celebrating Passover.

Why had Passover been lost? Satan had *stolen* it away! Satan always wants to steal Passover. As a new generation turned back to the Lord and began to read the Book of the Covenant, they read about Passover for the first time. It seemed strange to them. They said, "We've never done this!" (And that's exactly what we see in much of the church today.) But as the Holy Spirit moved on their hearts, they celebrated God's feast of redemption, and God's power and joy were restored.

THE CELEBRATION OF JESUS!

Passover is all about Jesus! He came as the Lamb of God! His blood redeems *us*. By His blood…judgment is turned away! By His blood…the power of the enemy is broken! By His blood…we are released from bondage and oppression. By His blood…we are set free to enter into God's promise!

Passover is the *Jesus* celebration! The more you understand Passover, the more you appreciate Jesus! If you don't understand Passover, you have a hard time fully understanding what Jesus did. As you celebrate Passover, you are declaring your faith in the power of His blood and His redemption. That's why one of the strangest things in the world is that Christians have accepted Satan's lie that Passover is not a "Christian" thing! We instead have not pressed past the egg hunt and the Easter bunny!

Satan tries to steal away Passover because he knows the

celebration of the blood releases power. Passover was stolen away from the church. But the good news is, God is *restoring* Passover!

All over the world churches are again celebrating Passover. And the *power* is returning! I invite you to celebrate the power of Jesus' blood. Join with Christians all over the world in the restoration of Passover. Passover was the first step in escaping the oppression of Egypt. Egypt was a place of absolute poverty, but Passover opened the door for escape. Passover allowed Israel to begin moving forward toward the abundant provision of the Promised Land. As you celebrate Passover, you begin to gain a mindset to prosper!

WHY DOES SATAN HATE PASSOVER?

Satan hates Passover because Passover is the celebration of Jesus. In *A Time to Prosper*, Robert Heidler and I share about this in more detail:

> When the Church gave up Passover, it invented other celebrations of Jesus (that's how we got Christmas and Easter). Of course, it's not bad to celebrate Jesus on those other days—it's always good to celebrate Christ! But the celebration of Jesus that *God* gave us is called Passover.
>
> The New Testament tells us that Jesus is the Passover Lamb. When John introduced Jesus, He said, "Behold! The Lamb of God who takes away the sin of the world!" (John 1:29, [NKJV]). Paul said, "Christ, our Passover lamb, has been sacrificed" (1 Cor. 5:7, NIV). In Revelation 4–5, we see all heaven joining together in what is essentially a huge Passover celebration honoring Jesus as the Lamb who was slain!
>
> Celebrating Passover *is* celebrating Jesus. As the Passover Lamb, He shed His blood to redeem us

from the enemy. When His blood is "on the door-post" of your life, God delivers you from the destroyer. Everything in Passover is a picture of Jesus, and every element points to Jesus!

Picture in your mind what took place on the original Passover night: The father of the house took the blood from the Passover lamb and put it in a bowl. He went to the door of his home, dipped a branch of hyssop into the blood, and applied it to the doorposts of the home. Then he dipped the hyssop into the blood again and reached up to apply blood to the lintel as well.

Now stop and picture what is taking place. First, the father takes the blood-dipped hyssop branch and moves it from side to side to apply blood to both door-posts. He then lowers the hyssop down into the bowl and reaches up over his head to apply blood to the lintel. Can you picture in your mind what this Israelite father is doing as he stands before the front door of his home? It's a gesture you've probably seen Roman Catholics do! Every father in Israel stood in front of his house and made the sign of the cross in the blood of the lamb. What a dramatic picture of Jesus! God's deliverance always comes by His cross and by His blood.

Through Passover, the Jews were redeemed out of the hand of the enemy. But Passover is also how *we* were redeemed! Passover is the celebration of redemption. As mentioned earlier, it was not by accident that Jesus died on Passover. God could have had Jesus die any time of year, but it was God's will for Him to die at Passover so we would recognize Him as our Passover Lamb.

Consider this again: Passover is so important to God that He chose to have the most important event in history—the death and resurrection of Jesus—take place at this time. God went to great lengths to *connect* the sacrifice of Jesus to Passover. This is interesting, because Constantine's goal was to *separate* the work of Jesus from Passover, while God's goal was to *connect* Jesus' work to Passover! God wants us to think of Jesus in the context of the Passover celebration.[6]

CELEBRATING PASSOVER

There is no one right way to celebrate Passover. Some purchase a copy of a Messianic Jewish Seder and go through all the elaborate rituals. This is a wonderful way to experience a Seder celebration, but it is not required. You can also observe Passover very simply, by sharing a meal and telling the Passover story, and then close by taking Communion to celebrate Jesus, our Passover Lamb. The primary goal is to remember the greatness of God's deliverance. As you complete your Passover celebration, be sure to thank God that you are redeemed out of every old cycle, that bondage is broken, that you are set free by the blood of the Lamb to enter the promise!

IS THIS PASSOVER THE SAME?

The coronavirus (COVID-19) that has spread around the globe is stirring worries in every country that global pandemics may now begin to reoccur. We might ask if this is our society's black plague. Aaron Schnoor shared:

> Looking at the history of epidemics offers a unique perspective on the coronavirus. Let's take a look at the numbers:

- Up to 200 million people died in Europe, Asia, and North Africa between 1331–1353 BC due to the bubonic plague.

- Up to 10 million people died in the Antonine Plague of Rome.

- 2 to 5 million people died in the Justinian Plague of 541 AD.

- Over 2 million people died in Iran during the 1772 Persian Plague.

- The influenza outbreak of 1918 killed somewhere between 50 million and 100 million people.

When you look at the events of the past, you see that the current coronavirus hardly compares to the size and scale of earlier pandemics. Unmentioned in the above list are outbreaks of smallpox, measles, typhus, cholera, HIV/AIDs, scarlet fever, yellow fever, and others—all of which killed thousands, in some cases millions, of people.[7]

To summarize, as we continue in this book, let us discover the power of the Lord's blood against any viral pandemic plague that is trying to rule the world and enter our homes.

CHAPTER 3

A New Era With a New Season of War

W E HOPE TO find reassurance in a quote often attributed to St. Francis of Assisi: "Start by doing what's necessary; then do what's possible, and suddenly you are doing the impossible."[1]

We have entered a new era where the impossible will become the norm! There is a moment when time makes a shift and you gain momentum for your future. We are in that kingdom moment now. We have entered not just a new year, decade, or season but a new era in the kingdom of God.

On October 11, 2018, in Chattanooga, Tennessee, I prophesied:

> This is what is ahead for two years and four months; you can mark it down today. We are coming through this place, we are coming through this swamp—and it is a swamp! We are in a time of breaking out of conventional ways of thinking. This is very key for us if we are going to make it through this place we are headed. With that, you have to understand we are making a shift in the harvest. It is not what we think. Anytime you are moving into a harvest season, the separation gets worse and worse and worse and greater and greater and greater. Over these next two years you will see one of the greatest separations in this nation. It will almost look like the Civil War has

come, but it's just that God is going to have to define this separation so we fully understand it. It will cause His people, filled with the Spirit, to rise up as one. It is what is going to happen with us—we won't have time for the racism issues or political squabbling. We won't have time for all of that because we're going to have to be ONE (in Him as His people). The voices with the anointing—we're going to have to learn to follow after the anointing and be able to see the anointing, because the separation is going to get greater and greater.

This prophetic word projects us into February 2021.

In Isaiah the Word of God says, "Look—a new era begins! A king will reign with righteousness, and his princes according to justice!" (Isa. 32:1, TPT). An era is a fixed point in time from which a series of years is reckoned. An era can also be a memorable or important date or event in the history of a thing, person, or nation. An era is a system of chronological notation computed from a given date as a basis. An era is a period identified by some prominent figure or characteristic feature or stage in development. *We have entered a new kingdom era.* In Hebrew this era is known as *pey*, which—as we have learned—means voice or mouth. As God's ambassadors, our voices must be heard in this decade.

We will decree a thing, and it will happen!

A TIME TO SEE, REFINE VISION, AND DECREE YOUR FUTURE

Without a vision a people perish. In Proverbs 29:18 this word actually means that without boundaries or prophetic utterance a people go backward. This is a critical point:

We are moving from a church *era to a* kingdom *era.*

In this divine shift the Lord is transforming our mindset so we move outwardly from what has been built in one season into a new movement for the next season. This will be a new building season, but first we must unlock God's kingdom plan and align heaven and earth.

When the Lord revealed His Messiahship to His disciples in Matthew 16, He gave Peter a prophetic word that would transcend the ages. In Matthew 16:18–19 (my paraphrase) He prophesied, "I will build My church, the gates of hell will not overpower it, and you will have authority to unlock the kingdom and forbid and permit what goes on in earth." We must remember that this prophecy to Peter had yet to be fully revealed in reality. *The church was still a mystery.* Therefore, when the day of Pentecost came and three thousand were converted, Peter must have thought, "How will we build for the future? How will the Lord, who has ascended, accomplish this through us?"

The disciples did not have a full concept of the meaning of the "church." The only concept they had of spiritual gathering was from the synagogue. The word the Lord was using here was *ecclesia*, which was a Roman concept of ambassadors going in to transform a region to make it look like Rome. Everything seemed new to the disciples. Just a few weeks prior, they had a revelation of the Lord being Messiah. Now they had to see how to gather and build for the future out of a new paradigm. Eventually they would have to leave Jerusalem to do this and build in Antioch a prototype of what the Lord was prophesying. The writer of Hebrews gave us much revelation of how what the Spirit of God was doing in that day could not be done in Jerusalem. This is an example of how God built in one season—in this instance how the church grew in Jerusalem and Judea—in order to move His church into a *new* season—and then to Antioch (modern-day southern Turkey) and to the uttermost ends of the earth.

This would begin a whole new era in the genesis of the early church. Now, the *Spirit of God* would help His leadership establish something that would be indestructible. There would be unsurpassed power in the ecclesia to overcome the enemy of mankind, Satan. But before the church was built, there had to be an unlocking of God's kingdom power within the triumphant people who would walk into the future. That is what the Book of Acts (in general) and Acts 2 (specifically) is all about: the church being imbued with the power and purposes of the Holy Spirit.

We must remember it took approximately seventy years to establish the first church era. In every era we unlock a kingdom plan so we can build the prototype for the ecclesia for the future. This new era propels us into a season of unlocking so that we can build in days ahead. That is exactly what God is doing—*right now.*

He is "passing over" His people, looking for His church—that body of believers who will be used in this *pey* decade of harvest in the midst of world turmoil. While this entire *pey* decade is strategic, there is a seven-year period—late fall 2019 through 2026—that will be *most critical.* During these seven years we will see great rearrangement of economic power structures as well as spiritual power shifts. Watch. Pray. (This will be discussed more in later chapters.) And when God releases you in your particular sphere and authority, move forward in boldness, not backward in fear.

A SEASON OF WAR!

We are living in conflicting and conflicted times. Many times the shifts we make are not our willful choices but result from the spiritual wars of the season. We would have loved to see something go one way, but atmospheric shifts in the spirit realm, conflicts of opinions, conflicts of philosophies, and conflicts of emotions caused things to go a different direction.

James said that we war because we have cravings and desires in us that cannot be satisfied (4:1). Many times these desires hold us in wilderness places. We are meant to cross over into prosperity, but we choose to have our way in a situation instead of submitting to the will of God. We are in a great warfare over a threefold cord controlled by Satan's kingdom consisting of poverty, infirmity, and religion.

War is the *grace to fight*. When the Lord calls us to war, He gives us the grace to triumph. God never calls His children to do anything without the grace that is necessary to fulfill His purpose. Therefore, in the midst of war, there is grace. We are called to protect our vineyard. My greatest concern for the church today is this: *Will a new generation rise up and war for all the promises that have been redeemed or paid for by the blood of the Lord Jesus Christ?*

Christians must learn why it's imperative that we fight and overturn the plans of the enemy. Learning to war comes easier to some than to others. To those who grew up in relative peace and comfort, it may come hardest of all. Why is war—particularly spiritual war—necessary? And more generally, why do nations and factions go to war? Why can't people live in harmony—spiritually, emotionally, relationally, even nationally?

These are the questions we ask our parents when we are first exposed to conflict through the media, in school, and playing with kids in the neighborhood. We ask the questions of our history teachers when we are learning the events that brought us to the present. Most importantly, we ask God, "If You are a loving God, why do war and destruction occur?"

The short answer is that there are two kingdoms in conflict. Satan's demonic angels roam the earth trying to keep his kingdom in place. We, however, belong to God's army of warriors. The Lord has already defeated Satan and all his dominions, powers, and principalities. However, we are called to enforce that defeat. If we do not heed His call, then the enemy will step in and rule in our stead. We are called to possess, secure, and protect our inheritance. We must remember that the earth is the Lord's and the fullness thereof! (See Psalm 24:1, KJV.)

As the Holy Spirit moves us toward becoming more Christlike, the methodology of an old season will *not* propel us into the future. We need something new and fresh. As our Lord inquired in Matthew 9:17, who puts new wine into an old, fragile wineskin? We need a new glory. This is one of the wiles of the enemy: to hold us captive in the last—former—manifestation of God. Therefore, we live in the past rather than move into the best that is ahead for our lives. This is how religious spirits operate: we become entrenched and enamored with past glory, our egos hold on to it, and the enemy takes advantage. Instead, God is calling us to let go so He can take us into the new season. Stop looking backward in longing toward the "leeks and onions of Egypt." (See Numbers 11:5.) He's delivered you from bondage, and you need to walk forward from your Passover!

HEAVEN AND EARTH MUST ALIGN

The Lord taught His disciples to pray using a model prayer, which we know as the Lord's Prayer from Matthew 6:9–13. We have access to the Father's throne room, but we must access the revelation for us to triumph and establish that in the earth realm. *The government of heaven must enter our atmosphere, align with the government of God in the earth, and liberate the armies of God and the land!*

IS PROPHECY FOR TODAY?

> And it shall come to pass in the last days, says God, that I will pour out of My Spirit on all flesh; your sons and your daughters shall prophesy, your young men shall see visions, your old men shall dream dreams.
>
> —ACTS 2:17, NKJV

The Spiritual Warfare Handbook is a compendium by Rebecca Wagner Sytsema and me that contains the wonderful book *When God Speaks*. We have a great section on understanding prophecy that is so helpful:

> Most Christians in the United States grew up in churches that did not embrace the idea of God speaking to us today. We were taught cessationism, which means that the power gifts of healing, tongues, interpretation of tongues, miracles and the like all ceased to function in the first century. One of the gifts that supposedly stopped functioning was prophecy. What that basically means is that God said all He had to say by AD 95 and has been silent ever since.
>
> Those who hold to this line of thinking believe that prophecy passed away when the Scriptures were completed. They base their belief on 1 Corinthians 13:8–9, which says that prophecy, tongues and knowledge will pass away. However, in the following chapter of 1 Corinthians, Paul encourages us to desire prophecy (see 14:1). He did not say that these gifts would be replaced by any others or that they would pass away before the Second Coming of Christ.
>
> In fact, in Ephesians 4 Paul writes: "And He Himself gave some to be apostles, some prophets, some evangelists, and some pastors and teachers, for

the equipping of the saints for the work of ministry, for the edifying of the body of Christ, *till we all come to the unity of the faith and of the knowledge of the Son of God, to a perfect man, to the measure of the stature of the fullness of Christ*" (vv. 11–13, NKJV, emphasis added). In this passage, we see that these gifts have been given *until* we come to unity and we reach the stature of the fullness of Christ. At no time in the history of the Church have we achieved these things. Therefore, based on Paul's own words, these gifts, including prophecy, are still in operation today.

HOW CAN WE KNOW THE WILL OF GOD?

The Bible makes it very clear that God has a purpose and a plan for our lives. Any biblical scholar will agree that this did not end in the first century. But if we have a God who doesn't speak to us, it will be hard to discern what that plan is. Many of us have read books or heard messages on knowing the will of God, which are filled with good principles to follow. Yet, the fact remains that the Bible only gives one real principle to follow in trying to determine God's will for our lives. In the Bible, when someone wanted to know the will of God, they asked Him—and He told them!

God *does* speak to His people. But if we are so entrenched in a mindset that says God does *not* speak today, we well write it off as our imagination. The truth is that the prophetic is not an optional extra in the Christian life or in the Church. Amos 3:7 goes so far as to say, "Surely the Lord GOD does nothing, unless He reveals His secret to His servants the prophets" [NKJV].[2]

In late 2019 the Lord had to find someone with whom He could discuss the year 2020. He had to say that this Passover season and the days, months, and decade beyond were crucial in His earth. Why did He decide to use me? I can't answer that—only the Lord can. My responsibility is simply to obey and try to bring forth the things He is sharing as accurately as I can.

The text of *When God Speaks* continues:

> In 1 Corinthians 12, Paul reminded the Gentiles that they once worshiped mute idols. What a foolish thing to worship something that cannot communicate! Our God, however, is not like the mute idols. Our God constantly pours out new revelation and is continually speaking to His people. He is a God who loves us enough to want to enter into communication with us.[3]

God speaks, and we prophesy what He says!

WHAT IS PROPHECY?

The definition of *prophecy* is simple. Prophecy is speaking the mind and heart of God as revealed by the Holy Spirit. Prophecy is the outflow of the heart and the very nature of God. Revelation 19:10 says that the testimony of Jesus is the spirit of prophecy. Jesus cares about His Church and therefore, has things He wants to communicate to His Church. Those communications come by way of the Holy Spirit. That is prophecy. It is what Jesus is saying to His Church. The testimony of Jesus, which is prophecy, is not just a corporate promise. Jesus says that His sheep know His voice (see John 10:4). If you are one of His sheep, you have the capability, the capacity and the privilege of hearing the voice of your Shepherd, which comes through the Holy Spirit.[4]

In the middle of a crisis, prophesy. This can come in the form of comfort, encouragement, exhortation, or direction. Never forget that there is a redemptive purpose in your life and surroundings that the Lord is unlocking. Prophesy that ultimate redemptive purpose.

NEW BATTLES AHEAD!

In August 2019 I spoke these words:

> What we are entering into is an era, a decade, called "speaking forth your liberty." We are going to see so much upheaval coming in the earth realm that you'll just have to hang on for dear life because there will be so many issues rearranged because of the voices that are coming forth. It's what the whole next decade is about, and each year will have a different significance of how we speak.

The last sentence is so key for us today. This year is 2020, but each of the nine years following will also have a major issue for us to contend for in battle.

While visiting Ghana on October 5–6, 2019, and being hosted by Archbishop Nicholas Duncan-Williams, I began to prophesy:

> This is what the season ahead looks like: Moses is just working the same way he's been working the last forty years. In the midst of his daily routine, a bush begins to burn. This interrupts Moses' life. Here is the key issue about this decade ahead—*God is going to interrupt our last season.* He is going to look at your last season, He is going to look at the last forty years, and

all of a sudden He is coming down in the midst of time and interrupting our times.

It is not unusual for bushes to burn out in the desert, but there is a faith action in Moses that is so important to what God is doing. The Word of God says that suddenly Moses "turned" to go look at the bush. God is going to be interrupting, but we're going to have to recognize the interruption. In the midst of that, we must turn and look at that bush and recognize it is not the same thing that "burned" last week or three years ago. Suddenly there is a divine interruption and Moses comes face to face with the bush, and God says, "Take your shoes off; you're in a new place." All of a sudden God reveals Himself to us and says, "I am ready for you to do some things that I've prepared you for forty years ago, but you weren't capable of completing them. Now I'm calling you into them and you'll be used to not only change a nation, but you'll be used to deliver a nation!" *The divine interruption is on the way!*

Catch the core of that word, dear friends: God is going to interrupt our last season, and we must be watchful to recognize His interruption. When He moves, we must be ready to "turn" and look at the new thing, the new season, as it will "burn" differently than it did in the past!

I HEAR A ROAR THIS YEAR!

"The Lord will thunder and roar from Zion" (Joel 3:16, AMPC)! From this scripture we developed the concept for our Head of the Year 5780 celebration, entering this new era with the roar of the Lord. During that gathering on September 26–29, 2019, I began to prophesy that the nations would come into turmoil until Passover. At Starting the Year Off Right 2020 on January 2–5, 2020, God was saying that there would be a massive upheaval that would test us through Passover. When I prophesied that in Las Vegas on January 26, 2020, I did get several comments and certain rebuttals for repeating that our nation would go into some sort of major trial through April. I believe that we are seeing this not only in this nation but throughout the world at this time in history.

In Joel 2 and 3 we find these statements:

> Fear not, O land; be glad and rejoice, for the Lord has done great things! Be not afraid, you wild beasts of the field, for the pastures of the wilderness have sprung up and are green…the fig tree and the vine yield their [full] strength. Be glad then, you children of Zion, and rejoice in the Lord, your God.
>
> —JOEL 2:21–23, AMPC

> Hasten and come, all you nations round about, and assemble yourselves; there You, O Lord, will bring down Your mighty ones (Your warriors). Let the nations bestir themselves and come up to the Valley of Jehoshaphat, for there will I sit to judge all the nations round about….Multitudes, multitudes in the valley of decision! For the day of the Lord is near in the valley of decision.
>
> —JOEL 3:11–12, 14, AMPC

On November 8, 2019, at a meeting here in Corinth, Texas, I heard the Lord say, "In DC there is a setup through man that has set structures in place, and you're going to start seeing tremendous death. Record the deaths, for when sin abounds, death abounds. Watch how I start causing certain dominoes to topple."

I said to the Lord, "What in the world will happen?"

He said: "Watch and stay in time with Me. Do not get distracted by any confused noise in the world. My divine interruption has begun!"

I didn't change my schedule or anything I was doing, but I began to watch the slightest situational changes around me.

I wrote a series of books based on when God visited me in 1986 and showed me four ten-year increments through 2026.[5] Everything we have just crossed over into in 2020 you will find in one of those books. Clearly 2020 will be our most intense year, and the nations will go into places of intensity they've never experienced before.

He showed me there would be divine alignments and moments of change that would produce faith explosions in His people. Get ready! Just as China, Russia, and America vie for power (to be discussed in following chapters), God says, "I have power within you that I will explode!" We will be in a great tension—a new era of warfare for us. It won't be like the warfare we've been in in the past. It's a tension arising that I call the Lion vs. the Dragon War.

That will happen this decade. We must know who we are part of. We must leave our maintenance mentality and walk into a conquest mentality based upon the boundaries God is assigning to each one of us. That is the word I want to leave with each one of us individually, corporately, territorially, and generationally.

My dear friend Cindy Jacobs was one of our ministers here on January 3, 2020, for our Starting the Year Off Right Celebration. She is with us here at the beginning of most years. She prophesied to me that during the first three months of this year, I would have to be cautious. I travel so much that I assumed she was referring to how much I fly. I had flown 570,000 miles in 2019 and was weary from all the travel and warfare.

Cindy actually shared that the Lord was saying that I needed rest, and I recognized the admonition for the first three months of 2020. Was this word ever correct! The Lord not only created a divine interruption in my life but also made sure that I entered into a well-needed Shabbat. Even though this January–March 2020 was a very intense time, I actually stopped most international travel during those three months and found an hour to sit before the Lord each day and converse with Him. As a result I began to feel new strength coming into my bones and new vision arising. Strength means the ability to withstand attack. This pause has helped create strength for me.

THE LORD IS REARRANGING OUR TIME AND SPACE

We need to submit in this rearrangement. The Lord says, "I am calling it a *pause*. Submit. Let the earth enter a time of Shabbat! The earth is Mine. Without a Shabbat, the fullness that I have planned for the future cannot manifest!"

Let's submit. Resist movement when God says to rest. Draw near to the Lord. If we do this, then we will see the enemy flee. This will help all of us to develop new mindsets, new ways of operation, and new thinking processes.

What is God saying to you at this pivotal time in history, at the dawn of a new decade? How does this pandemic fit into God's plan to interrupt our "old normal" (or old season) and to prepare us for the battle He has planned in the coming years? What is your role in the new season? Let's delve into these questions in the coming chapters.

CHAPTER 4

Tighten Your Belt: Economic Control vs. Transference of Wealth

I LIVE ON A covenant timetable and look at time through the Hebraic calendar—and not just the calendar but the way the Word of God is written around feast times. God built His covenant and time around harvest. He always wants us to have a harvest mentality. If we keep this type of mentality, we can always find our way into increase.

That is a real issue: How will we move back into increase after restrictions from the field have lifted?

TIGHTEN YOUR BELT

While I was spending time with the Lord on January 1, 2020, He spoke these words to me: "Tighten your belt!" I was perplexed and amazed. First of all, record economic projections were occurring. Prophets were predicting breakthrough. The world seemed to be running on course…but God! As I pursued His voice, I saw that this phrase could have several meanings:

- To see provision move toward a different dimension and the need to sacrifice and lower your standard of living

- To have less money today than in a preceding time period, which causes spending habits to change

- To reduce, restrict, or limit one's budget
- To live more modestly while you make financial sacrifices
- To spend less and live more carefully

"Tighten your belt" was a saying that came from the Depression era. I really pondered what I was hearing since when God says something like this, we must press in for more revelation. As I sought the Lord, He continued: "As My people enter a season of tightening their belts, I'm going to teach them to do exploits. This will start now!"

I knew there was a prophecy given to Daniel that said, "They who are wise and have spiritual insight among the people will instruct many and help them understand {and carry out great exploits}" (Dan. 11:33). However, I also knew that this prophecy was given in the prediction of a great stressful time to come.

To do exploits means we will take the resources that we steward and re-create those resources, bringing them into a new law of use. (I will explain this later in the chapter.) An *exploit* is a notable or heroic act. Therefore, these resources can be used productively for future accomplishments. Actually, this simply means to use something in a new way in our life ahead. I sensed the Lord was saying that in 2020 we were going to see great, incredible creativity and new levels of uses in all that belonged to us. However, there is also a negative connotation to exploitation. The other meaning of *exploit* is to unfairly use or take advantage of a situation. So I continued to seek the Lord.

A ROLLER-COASTER RIDE AHEAD!

Have you ever gone to an amusement park? Upon entering the roller-coaster ride, you hear these words: "Be sure to tighten your safety belt." Remembering this phrase made me ask, "Are we headed into a roller-coaster-type year in the financial economic realm?" By using the roller-coaster analogy, the Lord was attempting to reveal to me how to tighten up for the ride ahead—both up and down. Some drops would be worse than others. The emotion generated from a roller coaster can be glee and joy or terror and horror. Some drops are worse than others. A friend asked me recently about the stock market. I told him about the roller coaster. I said, "Only when the car hits the bottom of the drop should you buy."

A NEW THING HAS BEGUN—THE DIVINE RESET

As we enter a new era, we must consider what Isaiah said: "Behold, I am doing a new thing; now it springs forth, do you not perceive it?" (Isa. 43:19, ESV). This emphasizes to us that we can miss what is happening around us and not fully understand the time. For those with perception, it will be difficult to miss what God is saying and doing.

We are going to be desperate as we move through 2020 and into 2021.

Desperation and crisis create a move of God. What really happens in a new era is that all of a sudden you're at the end and the beginning at the same time. You have to go through a reset, like rebooting a computer. Some things you can't comprehend or understand—especially when they go wrong and there seems to be no easy solution. Therefore, the easiest thing to do is turn the computer off and turn it back on again. This is called a reset. Restarting your computer dumps a level of cached junk. Then everything starts working and comes back into a new order. The Lord says, "I am resetting the glitches of your past season. I am getting ready to put you in a new motion and order to speak your future."

As kingdom people we must understand this is where the Spirit of God now has us in the earth realm. We must always hear what the Spirit of God is saying to the church. Because of our current situation, this should become a model for our future. Several interpretations could be given over the situation of COVID-19 as havoc has occurred throughout the nations. Some would even say that this virus has stopped any movement where revival can continue. We must all assess the signs of change and what we should be perceiving!

THE DIVINE PAUSE—GIRD YOUR LOINS

Over the past few years I visited Las Vegas approximately four times a year because of the wonderful International Church of Las Vegas. And each time I would say, "It isn't the gambling and all the indecency in this city that offends the Lord. There is a great harvest here for salvation. Like anywhere, the people serve and live the best they can. However, the Lord does have one major problem: there is never a Shabbat, a pause. He rested one day out of seven, and this city here never rests." Beginning in mid-March, however, the city streets of Las Vegas became empty and quiet—paused by the hand of God.

God has caused a pause until He sees who is willing to cross over with Him through His blood at Passover.

This Passover has become a dividing line for our future. Susan Stanfield, who has worked with me for almost forty years, shared that the Lord told her to "gird up your loins for spring storms ahead." What the Lord spoke to me at the beginning of 2020 about the need for the church to "tighten your belts" is the same principle as girding up your loins. Therefore, I knew this would be a hard financial year but that we would enter into the greater as we kept pressing forward. If we would choose to gird up our loins, then we would end up doing exploits.

To ensure proper alignment, weight lifters "gird their loins" with special belts that strengthen and support the lower back and core when there is a heavy load on the spine. I talked to Joshua Aubrey, a weight-lifting champion on our pastoral staff. He works in our gym, training individuals to become more physically fit. He has a twelve-week program to help people lose twenty pounds and "tighten their belts." (I have yet to enroll in this program.) Joshua is presently on this program and is currently "between notches." The last notch is too loose, and the next one is still a bit tight. This probably sums up our economy right now!

Another belt or fastening article that characterized a soldier's dress was termed the waistband or gird of strength. God challenges the nations to gird themselves for battle. Sometimes the military significance is replaced by a more general call to "prepare for action." Girding your loins can also mean preparing for controversy that is pending. When God turned David's mourning into dancing, He girded (clothed) him with gladness (Ps. 30:11, KJV). A similar metaphor characterizes the Messiah, who wears righteousness and truth around His waist (Isa. 11:5, NLT).

In *Restoring Your Shield of Faith*, Robert Heidler and I write: "We are to gird ourselves with truth. This weapon is that which is reliable and can be trusted. The Bible uses truth in the general factual sense. Truth may designate the actual fact over appearance, pretense or assertion. In Zechariah 8:16 (NRSV), the Lord of Hosts declared: 'These are the things that you shall do: Speak the truth to one another, render in your gates judgements that are true and make for peace.'"[1]

PROPHETS MUST GIRD UP!

Prophets must always stay girded and ready to advance. During such seasons of quarantine (or perhaps recent quarantine), lack of travel, and lockdown, I have watched prophets gather through Zoom, an online vehicle. Many key prophets have come together to discuss what the Lord is showing them for the future. This is normal for prophets. The Lord told Elijah to gird up for the fight ahead with Jezebel. Jeremiah was instructed, "Gird up thy loins, and arise, and speak unto them all that I command thee: be not dismayed at their faces, lest I confound thee before them" (Jer. 1:17, KJV).

Most of all, I love what Yeshua taught: "Blessed are those servants, whom the lord when he cometh shall find watching: verily I say unto you, that he shall gird himself, and make them to sit down to meat, and will come forth and serve them" (Luke 12:37, KJV). Peter, the disciple who became a leading apostle, had to learn hard lessons that then allowed him to teach lessons for generations to come: "Wherefore gird up the loins of your mind, be sober, and hope to the end for the grace that is to be brought unto you at the revelation of Jesus Christ" (1 Pet. 1:13, KJV).

Recently Anne Tate, an apostolic watchman here at Global Spheres Center, prophesied: "Be gathered to Me this week and see My belt come around you as the body of Christ, and I will tighten it, and I will pour My strength into you for this battle. What is ahead is not too much for My people, but I will cause nations to stagger."

As Anne reviewed this word, I asked her to write up what she was hearing:

> Once Chuck had prophesied about "tighten your belt" and the call to gird up your loins, I started working on

understanding a greater portion of the meaning. The Lord initially gave me the word *stagger* because several intercessors had experienced vertigo, which is supposed to be the first sign of the Coronavirus according to some medical reports. In Job 12 I found this: "He pours contempt on princes and nobles and loosens the belt of the strong [disabling them]. He uncovers mysteries [that are difficult to grasp and understand] out of the darkness and brings back gloom and the shadow of death into light. He makes nations…and leads them away [captive]. He removes intelligence and understanding from the leaders of the people of the earth and makes them wander and move blindly in a pathless waste. They grope in darkness without light. And He makes them stagger like a drunken man" (Job 12:21–25).

In Isaiah 45:1 we find, "This is what the LORD says to His anointed, to Cyrus [king of Persia], whose right hand I have held to subdue nations before him, and I will ungird the loins of kings [disarming them]; to open doors before him so that gates will not be shut" (Isa. 45:1)! I also looked this up in The Passion Translation, and the footnote for Isaiah 45:1 shares: "'The belts of their kings I will loosen' [is] a Hebrew idiom for disarming or dethroning. Babylon was taken in one night by Cyrus. Belshazzar, the Chaldean king, was killed." Either nations will be tightening their belts or God will be loosening their belts. Many nations will become ungirded and stagger during this time of trial that is affecting the world.[2]

Anne concluded:

> We have this Passover 2020 in common with the
> children of Israel. God showed me places where I
> personally needed to repent and be freshly circum-
> cised. He showed me structures that were in place
> in former times for Israel that are now in place in
> His people and our culture. Here are two things He
> showed me that I felt were important to share. The
> Lord said, *"My altar is where every triumph is secured
> or remains in jeopardy."* I saw the Lord manifesting
> His altar in our innermost parts. God also said, *"You
> will recognize Pharaoh structures now by their hard-
> ness of heart."* He showed me faces of buildings
> or structures with crossed arms and holding dark
> scrolls in their hands. On the scrolls were construc-
> tion plans of enemies standing in agreement. I saw
> the Lord breaking the seals of the scrolls of those
> with no altars to Him. Once this occurred, He made
> them appear dark.[3]

Recent reports show the impact that is now occurring as
follows:

> Coronavirus-induced shockwaves are rippling through
> the world economy, causing tremendous damage that
> we are only just beginning to measure.... The small/
> medium-sized enterprises (SMEs) like your local res-
> taurant, dry cleaner, bookstore and building con-
> tractor are being hit especially hard.... Many may
> never reopen.... It's certain that we're heading into
> recession. How deep and long [will] it be? Will the
> announced stimulus efforts help? Can we get things

back to the way they were, or are we entering a "new normal"?[4]

THE PLAGUE OF DAVID'S CENSUS

In America 2020 is a census year. This reminded me of a Bible story set during David's time. David made several mistakes; however, he always had a heart after the Lord. One of his worst mistakes was taking a census and numbering the people. What was the real problem with this action, since all through the Word of God we find censuses being taken? When you read the account of David's census in 2 Samuel 24, you find that a pestilence or plague struck the people, resulting in many deaths. David was cautioned by several people not to take this census. In doing so, he relied on man's strength and cut off heaven's power and all the hosts and armies of heaven.

How did he do this?

He had forgotten the word and edict that was given to Moses in Exodus 30:11–16, called the law of ransom. Moses had instructed that when you take a census, you bring an offering. This would always connect the people with the One who was their God. David had forgotten this step. In Exodus 30:13–15 everyone subject to the census (over twenty years of age) was to pay the exact same amount of one-half a shekel, about one-fifth of an ounce of silver. This was not a large sum. The rich did not pay more, and the poor did not pay less. Hebraic sources tell us this was because it was not the individual people who were numbered but the ransom itself, which is why it had to be the same amount for everyone.

This is such a picture of our corporate identity—that we are all of equal value in the Lord's community and that, to function as a body, we must all give of ourselves. Another sobering reason for counting the people corporately rather than as individuals was because according to rabbinic tradition, "the evil eye has power over numbered things." Within a corporate identity each of us is part of a whole, not a numbered individual. This causes me to rejoice in the protection found in the body.

Not coincidentally, the Hebrew expression for *number* is a *pey* word, *paqad*. This word means to attend, to muster, to visit (for blessing or punishment), to appoint, and to care for.[5] When the tribes were numbered, the strength of their armies was assessed. We have entered a decade when the Lord of hosts is assessing the strength of His armies throughout the earth—from region to region and nation to nation. In the Passover context this word was used in Exodus 3 when God visited the people to see what was happening to them in Egypt. Today I see that not only does the Lord number us to assess our strength, but He is also visiting to remove iniquity, recompense past oppression, and bring forth our future.

Once David got in God's order, he built an altar and gave an offering to the Lord, and the plague stopped. Yeshua said, "When you come together, remember Me!" (See Luke 22:19.) In this census year if we worship, give, and commune, the angelic hosts will align with God's army in the earth, and we will win the wars ahead!

LESSONS FROM THE BLACK PLAGUE

In a time of great uncertainty there is great wisdom in reviewing the history of how we have come to this place. A March 4, 2020, *National Interest* article puts it this way:

> While the plague that caused the Black Death was very different to the coronavirus that is spreading today,

there are some important lessons for future economic growth....

It might sound counter-factual—and this should not minimise the contemporary psychological and emotional turmoil caused by the Black Death—but the majority of those who survived went on to enjoy improved standards of living. Prior to the Black Death, England had suffered from severe overpopulation....

The [English] government's immediate response was to try to hold back the tide of supply-and-demand economics.... The Statute of Labourers law was passed in 1351 in an attempt to peg wages to pre-plague levels and restrict freedom of movement for labourers. Other laws were introduced attempting to control the price of food and even restrict which women were allowed to wear expensive fabrics. But this attempt to regulate the market did not work. *Enforcement of the labour legislation led to evasion and protests*. In the longer term, real wages rose as the population level stagnated with recurrent outbreaks of the plague....

There was *large-scale migration* after the Black Death as people took advantage of opportunities to move to better land or pursue trade in the towns. Most landlords were forced to offer more attractive deals to ensure tenants farmed their lands. *A new middle class of men (almost always men) emerged*. These were people who were not born into the landed gentry but were able to make enough surplus wealth to purchase plots of land.... The dramatic population change wrought by the Black Death also led to an *explosion in social mobility*. Government attempts to restrict these developments followed and generated tension and resentment.[6]

GREED OR THE TRANSFERENCE OF WEALTH?

Whether we look at individuals or governments, we recognize it is human nature to want more. In 2007's *God's Unfolding Battle Plan* I wrote:

> Yet in America, we have reached an all-time materialistic high—or should I say low? For decades, American culture has known nothing but plenty. We are a nation bursting at the seams with a belief in the almighty dollar—and why not? Those who can recall the lean years of the Great Depression are literally a dying generation. We have enjoyed abundance for so long that we now equate happiness with a fully loaded 401(k) and a diversified financial portfolio. That, of course, and a comfortable piece of real estate, the latest shiny SUV and all the high-tech gadgets a credit card can hold. Clearly, our desire is out of alignment.
>
> What is the Church to do in a culture enamored with possessions? Christ explicitly and repeatedly taught about the dangers of the love of money. In fact, we have all probably sat through enough sermons on tithing, giving or financial stewardship to know that money is a big deal to God. It is the one subject Jesus spoke about more than any other. And yet, as Christians, we have typically responded one of two ways to money throughout history: We have either looked down on it, holding up poverty and meagerness as the higher path to Kingdom living, or we have fallen in love with it, using an assortment of biblical misinterpretations to justify a lifestyle of excess.[7]

Interestingly I wrote those words just before the financial crisis hit the US in late 2007. What is God trying to tell us now, during a tumultuous economic time that is hitting the US—and world—economies harder than the one in 2007–2008? Not since World War II have we seen the world in such a state of turmoil.

In light of economic crisis and uncertainty, we must keep our eyes fixed on biblical patterns and concepts. It is important, then, to remember that increase is a harvest principle. The Hebrew word for *building, banah,* signifies the adding of sons and daughters so that the plan of God can be passed from one generation to another. Increase rises through faith and follows effort and deeds linked with faith. Increase also comes through connecting with one another. When we are linked together, when we eschew independence, we gain strength in multiplied corporate measure. Increase is also a reward for obedience. There is joy in obedience, and the joy of the Lord causes our strength to increase. (See Colossians 1:9–11 and Nehemiah 8:10.) With such strength we are capable of building according to God's strategic plan for the future.

An incredible history book called *The Wealth and Poverty of Nations: Why Some Are So Rich and Some So Poor* by David S. Landes is a study of empires and how they gain wealth. Landes is an optimist. Even though many economic experts warn of depression, poverty, war, disease, and ecological disaster—the horsemen of the apocalypse riding in to bring destruction—he believes there is an incredible future ahead, and I agree with his assessment. Where we differ is that I believe our future is in a holy God who wants His covenant plan accomplished on earth.

WATCHMEN NEED TO WATCH!

Throughout history the use of wealth has changed, and it will continue to change. However, wealth never goes away; wealth is transferred and redistributed for stewardship. In the midst of the crisis that has occurred with this worldwide economic stall, watchmen need to rise up to watch over the provision that is necessary for the kingdom of God to move ahead with the work of missions, evangelism, and church activity. While salvation is free, the work of God's people in this world takes economic funding. Have no doubt, during this time of great change, when people's hearts are more open than usual to the love of Yeshua, the enemy will make a play to gain control of wealth. He will do this through greedy people who are in operation throughout the nations. We must bind the strong man.

BINDING THE STRONG MAN

In Matthew 12:22–29 our Lord addressed the Pharisees concerning the deliverance of a man who had been blind and mute. The Pharisees accused Jesus of being part of the ruling demon structure that had blinded the man. But Jesus reminded them that a kingdom divided against itself cannot stand. If Jesus were of Satan's own kingdom, then by casting out demons, Satan's own kingdom would be made powerless. Jesus' works, He explained, demonstrated that in fact the kingdom of God was among them. Then He set forth an interesting principle in verse 29 (NASB): "Or how can anyone enter the strong man's house and carry off his property, unless he first binds the strong man? And then he will plunder his house."

Jesus' illustration ties into prosperity and wealth. First He is showing us that there is a strong man that rules Satan's kingdom in any territory. This is where we see the Lord beginning to define the hierarchical structure of Satan's kingdom. But the interesting principle is that if we bind the strong man, we can plunder his house and take his spoils. Apostolic authority arises throughout the earth and aligns with strategic prophetic intercession through spiritual warfare. As this authority comes forth, I believe we will plunder the enemy's kingdom, and we can unlock the wealth necessary for the kingdom harvest in days ahead.

Many economic changes have occurred—and continue to occur—in these days. Here are some things we must watch for:

1. The bubble has burst. As the worth of assets rose, people continued to borrow and gain leverage. This is going to shift drastically.

2. Central banks will tighten monetary policies, and money will not be as freely lent as in the past.

3. A great wealth gap has now formed. Strong-minded leaders who are nationalistic will now arise with great power and gain control. I will explain more of this when I write on the nations realigning in chapters 5 and 6.

4. The education system as we know it must be completely reevaluated. The debt structures in the education system must be forgiven in some measure and be restructured for the future.

5. We must unlock a new level of productivity and produce new opportunity for the future. This will be like any effort after wartime.

6. Selling debt worldwide will become a great problem. This could last as much as the next three years. With debt, you are promising to pay an amount in a certain time. Because of the current unemployment situation, the prospect of paying debt looks difficult for us in days ahead.

7. The dollar will be reevaluated. Therefore, debt structures must fully change. Cash flow will become very restricted. This will produce a debt crisis.

8. Industrial diversification is vital.

9. The Federal Reserve System (the central bank of the United States) must be watched carefully.

10. We must stay open-minded and creative.

In this current crisis we must find out how to equalize and help more people than usual. I like what the Word of God says: there is a jubilee that should be entered into and celebrated. After forty-nine years of great debt there came a release of debt and a rearrangement of assets. There should be a forgiveness of debt issued in America especially. Instead of nations vying for control, they could begin to work together over debt issues.

THE POOR WILL ALWAYS BE WITH YOU

Giving is key! When Judas got upset over an offering that Mary gave Jesus, the Lord said, "The poor you will always have with you, but you will not always have me" (Matt. 26:11, NIV). What we understand is creative giving. We must not give haphazardly during the changes ahead but give purposefully. There is a disparaging saying that applies in most adverse situations that a nation encounters: "The rich get richer and the poor get poorer." Wealthy nations marginalize the poor for being poor. This has created major pockets of bondage and slavery, especially in large cities.

Rising from the bottom can be very difficult. Yet we love entertainment and pay greatly for those who entertain us. In a moment a young college student can become a multimillionaire if he or she has skills to display to the public. A person with great talent can increase thirty-, sixty-, or one hundredfold. (See

Luke 19 and Matthew 13:8.) This is also a principle and law of stewardship. However, we must always stop and ask, "Why am I being favored?" The Lord has ways to awaken us to the disparities around us.

Yes, the poor will always be with us, but we must never lose our compassion to give of what we have been given to increase the life flow of others. We must develop ways to keep transforming the societal structure around us.

THERE WILL BE AN OPENING FOR FUNDING THAT PROPELS A KINGDOM ADVANCEMENT

In this national emergency we should start looking at things more philanthropically. Let's look at Passover time in Egypt. Moses instructed the people to ask their Egyptian neighbors for articles of silver, gold, and clothing. It's fascinating to note that the Egyptians complied, despite the fact that they were clearly grieving over their dead.

God certainly gave the Jews favor just before they left Egypt, as the Bible says in Exodus 12: "The LORD gave the people favor in the sight of the Egyptians, so that they gave them what they asked. And so they plundered the Egyptians [of those things]" (v. 36).

As we have come through Passover 2020, I believe we are entering a season of special favor. As you cross over, always ask the Lord to give you favor for your supply ahead. He knows what you need to use for your journey as you proceed forward each year.

WE MUST LEARN TO DO EXPLOITS: GAINING A MINDSET OF MULTIPLICATION AND USE

As I said earlier, the real issue is how we will move from crisis back to prosperity. When this viral crisis began to produce many restrictions, my first thought was, "How will the many widows that we minister to be taken care of?" Currently we have about 340 widows that we watch after and try to give to quarterly. We are always available to them if they have needs. I knew that I needed to write a letter to the widows and send them an offering to help alleviate the need for them to go in and out of their homes as much during a time of quarantine. When we send to every widow at one time, that is a considerable amount of money. I refused to allow any sort of fear to attack my mind over the future but knew that if I would just bless the widows, we would be blessed.

God is bringing us through some hard times. He wants you to know He is with you and has a plan for your life. The best is yet ahead! Never give in to defeatism. A good example of this comes from 2 Kings 4. This chapter contains a story of a woman in debt and crisis after the death of her husband.

> A certain woman of the wives of the sons of the prophets cried out to Elisha, saying, "Your servant my husband is dead, and you know that your servant feared the LORD. And the creditor is coming to take my two sons to be his slaves."
>
> So Elisha said to her, "What shall I do for you? Tell me, what do you have in the house?" And she said, "Your maidservant has nothing in the house but a jar of oil."
>
> Then he said, "Go, borrow vessels from everywhere, from all your neighbors—empty vessels; do not gather just a few. And when you have come in, you shall shut the door behind you and your sons; then pour it into all those vessels, and set aside the full ones."
>
> So she went from him and shut the door behind her and her sons, who brought the vessels to her; and she poured it out. Now it came to pass, when the vessels

> were full, that she said to her son, "Bring me another vessel."
>
> And he said to her, "There is not another vessel." So the oil ceased. Then she came and told the man of God. And he said, "Go, sell the oil and pay your debt; and you and your sons live on the rest."
>
> —2 Kings 4:1–7, NKJV

The prophet Elisha showed this woman a kingdom principle: the principle of multiplication. Elisha asked the widow, "What can I do for you?" The Lord is still asking this question today. God had a plan to bring this widow into His blessing and to meet the deepest desires of her heart, and He has the same goal for you.

In Mark 6:32–44 we find a similar story, in which Jesus had compassion on a large crowd. He had been teaching them many things, and when it grew late in the day, He told His disciples to give them something to eat.

> But He answered and said to them, "You give them something to eat."
>
> And they said to Him, "Shall we go and buy two hundred denarii worth of bread and give them something to eat?"
>
> But He said to them, "How many loaves do you have? Go and see."
>
> And when they found out they said, "Five, and two fish."
>
> Then He commanded them to make them all sit down in groups on the green grass. So they sat down in ranks, in hundreds and in fifties. And when He had taken the five loaves and the two fish, He looked up to heaven, blessed and broke the loaves, and gave them to His disciples to set before them; and the two fish He

> divided among them all. So they all ate and were filled.
> And they took up twelve baskets full of fragments and
> of the fish. Now those who had eaten the loaves were
> about five thousand men.
>
> —MARK 6:37–44, NKJV

When God asks, "What can I do for you?" He's saying He wants to bless you. In Romans 8:32 Paul tells us, "If God loved you enough to send His own Son to die for you, there's no good thing that He will withhold" (author's paraphrase). The word *blessing* means to cause to increase. A curse brings decrease, while a blessing brings increase. If we are walking in God's blessing, we should always be increasing. To increase is to prosper.

During the Dark Ages most of the church bought into the philosophy of asceticism, which said that God is happier when we are poor. Those who wanted to please God were told to take a vow of poverty. But that philosophy is not in the Bible. Almost all of the people we read about in God's Word were prosperous. Abraham was one of the wealthiest men in the land. Isaac, Jacob, and Joseph prospered as well. David, Daniel, and Paul were great men of God, and they were successful.

God wants you to be successful as well. He wants you to prosper and succeed in everything He has called you to do. That is His will, and that is His promise. You are not to worship money or let it control your life—the love of money will always get you in trouble. But God is not against money! He doesn't want His children to walk in poverty and His church to be hindered by lack.

THE LAW OF MULTIPLICATION

One well-known example of the law of multiplication in physics is Newton's law of universal gravitation. This states that "every point mass in the universe attracts every other point mass with a force that is directly proportional to the product of their masses and inversely proportional to the square of the distance between them."[8] What happens if we violate this law of gravity? Obviously one object will hit another with great velocity!

There are spiritual laws of multiplication and prosperity just like physical laws, and these laws work the same way. Just because there is a worldwide crisis does not mean these laws have changed or will change. In the midst of this outbreak we still do not want to violate any of these laws. When we violate one of the laws, instead of increasing we decrease; and instead of multiplying, we stay the same, divide, or dwindle. In *A Time to Prosper*, Robert Heidler and I share about the biblical patterns and laws that will favor us. Here are some of the laws of multiplication:

1. *The Law of Use—debt can be overcome through exploits.* (See 2 Kings 4.) Recognizing authority assures security. Notice in this story how [the] woman recognized the authority of the prophet and his ability to gain revelation that would cause [her] to increase. (We will discuss this law further in the next section.)

2. *The Law of Firstfruits—the best produces the rest.* (See 1 Kings 17; Genesis 14; Acts 4.) (For further understanding, see *A Time to Advance.*)

3. *The Law of Discipleship—learn to be a disciple of love.* (See Matthew 14:13–21.) When John the Baptist was beheaded, Jesus pulled aside to seek the Father over how to shift His disciples to a new level of authority. The beheading of John represented the end of a forerunner

season and the maturing of the next wine-skin. The first lesson the Lord taught His disciples was a lesson on multiplication. They wanted Him to feed the 5,000 people who were following Him. Instead, He said, "You feed them!" He then activated the Law of Use in His teaching and had them bring Him the fish and loaves of a little boy. He broke the food into pieces, multiplied what was there and fed all the people. He taught His disciples that His love for the people could multiply the resources available.

4. *The Law of Persistence—keep on and you will receive.* (See Luke 11:9–13; 18:1–8.) The persistent widow did not relent in petitioning the judge until she received favor to get what she needed. Ask and keep on asking, seek and keep on seeking, and knock until the door opens.

5. *The Law of Waste—pour out in devotion.* (See John 12:1–8.) Mary poured out her savings and retirement. This seemed a waste, but it secured the future for mankind. Sometimes, when you pour out what you have, the Lord multiplies grace back to you.

6. *The Law of Giving—give out of love.* (See John 3:16.) God gave so that we could multiply in grace. Jesus taught giving. The apostles taught giving. Giving breaks the curse of robbing from God and opens the heavens.

7. *The Law of Worship—worship in faith to go higher.* (See Genesis 22:1–19.) In *The Worship*

> *Warrior,* John Dickson and I explain how
> faith and worship work together. I believe this
> is our most important law. Learn to ascend in
> worship. Abraham ascended Mount Moriah
> for his faith to be tested. He worshiped, and
> this caused a revelation of God to come
> strongly into the atmosphere. The provision
> was there. After Abraham worshiped, he could
> see his provision for the future.[9]

THE LAW OF USE

If we are going to understand doing "exploits," then we must understand the law of use. This is a very interesting principle. *Use* employs something for a specific purpose. *Use* takes something that is available for consumption and makes that item or resource active. As we discuss in *A Time to Prosper,* the following are some principles from the Word that utilize the law of use:

- *Give to someone more legitimate than you.* (See Genesis 14.) Giving is a major faith action to activate the law of use. Abraham knew he had gained resources and spoils from war. However, instead of keeping what he had won, he presented all the spoils as an offering to Melchizedek, the high priest. He gave to someone more legitimate than himself. When he used these resources as firstfruits, God made a covenant with him shortly thereafter. (See Genesis 15.)

- *Outline your future.* (See Genesis 22; 25:23; 27:29; and 28:3–4, 13–15.) The Lord knows your future. You should be reviewing your future with Him. The word *future* means "expected end." He already has an end planned for you. This is where vision originates from.

Out of vision comes provision. If we outline our future, we know what resources are available to us. We can then use those resources to advance.

- *Watch for angelic assistance.* (See Genesis 28:12, Exodus 23:20–24, and Luke 2:8–14.) Angels are sent as messengers and helpers on our path. When we listen and use the revelation and protection they bring, we triumph. They can lead us into new places of provision.

- *Remember your commitments to serve.* (See Genesis 28:18–19.) Once we make a vow, we need to use the power in that vow to serve until the promise that the vow is connected to manifests.

- *Remember the memorial events in your life.* (See Genesis 28:20–22 and Haggai 1–2.) When we use a portion of our resources to give as a memorial offering, God shakes loose the best that is ahead for us.

- *Be willing to operate in the principle of firstfruits giving, even in your need.* (See 1 Kings 17:8–16.) The widow first gave to the prophet what she had. He knew how to use this offering to multiply and sustain them for several days.

- *Evaluate your resources and enter into a new level of creativity.* (See 2 Kings 4.) The prophet asked another widow what she had in her house to use. This was after asking her what she wanted him to do for her. He took what she had, gave her a strategy, and she paid off all of her debt.

- *Give to an anointing greater than yours.* (See 2 Kings 4 and 8.) The woman of Shunem was rich. However, she used a portion of her home and belongings for the prophet. This broke barrenness and death from her and caused the law of restoration to work on her behalf later.

- *Let love be your motivator.* (See John 3:16.) God the Father used His best to give so that mankind would be redeemed.

- *Everything you steward should multiply.* (See Luke 19.) We must never let fear keep us from using what God has given to us to multiply. How we use our resources is proportionate to our judgment and increase. Do not let fear increase![10]

Crisis causes us to learn to manage resources differently. We learn the law of multiplication. We operate in the law of use. And in the next several years we will learn to do exploits!

CHAPTER 5
First Testing, Then Triumph

I Kings 18:37

AMERICA HAS GONE through many difficult times. But in the midst of all her troubles this nation has attempted to remain aligned with Israel. During President Obama's eight-year tenure, there was an attempt to become to anti-Israel, but the Lord intervened. President Donald Trump has been the most vocal pro-Israel president in many decades and definitely the boldest worldwide. On December 6, 2017, President Trump formally recognized Jerusalem as the capital of Israel, reversing nearly seven decades of American foreign policy, and set in motion a plan to move the United States Embassy from Tel Aviv to the fiercely contested Holy City. He stated, "Today we finally acknowledge the obvious: that Jerusalem is Israel's capital....This is nothing more or less than a recognition of reality. It is also the right thing to do. It's something that has to be done"![1]

PROPHECY CREATES DIVERSE REACTIONS: THE FUTURE WAR OF THE CHURCH AND 9/11

I wrote a book in 2000 about the future of the church in world society. As mentioned earlier, the Lord had visited me in 1986 and showed me ten-year increments of world events and how the church must respond through 2026. I will share more in the following chapter, especially relating to China and the present world predicament. *The Future War of the Church,* coauthored with

Rebecca Wagner Sytsema, was published by Regal Books and released in October 2000. There was an antiwar sentiment settling on the church at that time, which caused the book to create some controversy.

In January 2001 I wrote and published a prophecy about how America would be in war by September 2001. The Lord said that the first attack would come in New York, because at that time more Jews lived there than in Israel. I thought all would want to know this. However, this resulted in more warfare and controversy and culminated with a leader standing up in a meeting in Mississippi on September 10 to tell me that I was leading the body of Christ astray with such nonsense. Only a day later we witnessed the attack on the Twin Towers of the World Trade Center.

Justin Rana is a longtime assistant of mine and currently serves as our director of media and communication. As I began writing this chapter, he reminded me of what happened on our flight to Baltimore to the International School of Prophets in February 2001:

> In my role at Glory of Zion International, it is part of my duty to pay attention to what is being said so I can help distribute the message to the globe through our various channels of communication. Over the course of my life at GZI, I have realized how important it is to live by the timing and voice of God. We can all hear Him. We can all be sensitive to Holy Spirit and live in a measure of faith that will cause us to stay in His timing. However, in times like this, faith can falter. If you are like me, you don't like to simply ignore what is going on in the world. You like to stay abreast to see the schemes and plans that are being hatched. The schemes of the enemy are many. Staying

in faith becomes even more of a daily battle. It's very similar to another time in history.

Flash back to the year 2001. I was twenty years old and had just started serving full-time with Glory of Zion International under Apostle Chuck Pierce. I had been part of the worship team since I was fifteen years old and had been traveling to national conferences since 1998. In February 2001 we were slated to travel to Baltimore, Maryland, for a conference put on by Global Harvest Ministries at Bart Pierce's church, Rock City Church. Rebekah Pierce (now Faubion), Sam Dickson, John Dickson, LeAnn Squier and others were all a part of this traveling team. It was a great group. At some point in the flight to Baltimore, Apostle Chuck passed us in the aisle on his way to the bathroom. A few minutes passed, then Chuck came back, but he looked quite different—like he had been "visited," and not necessarily in a good way. We found out a bit later that God was giving him a vision. Chuck shared the vision with a few people when we landed in Baltimore: "I saw terrorists taking over planes and crashing them into Washington, DC." My first ignorant thoughts as a twenty-year-old young man? "Chuck is going to ruin this trip!" And honestly, it did! We went into such a place of intensity that it was *not* fun—a harbinger of things to come.

Over the next several months, Chuck began to share in pieces what the Lord was showing him and that the church needed to prepare for war. If you remember what life was like at that time, you will know that sharing a message about "preparing for war" was met with a lot of resistance and accusation about scaring people. People were very comfortable. They liked the lives they led. This sounds very familiar to how things were a couple months ago in America—but I digress.

Move ahead to September 5, 2001. Chuck had written a book called *The Future War of the Church,* and a movement was beginning to form around it. The same team that had gone to Baltimore was slated to travel to Virginia Beach, Virginia, for a conference named after the book. It was an intense conference. We flew back from Virginia and prepared to do the next "Future War of the Church" conference that was slated for California on September 20–22. God knew the timing and prophetic significance of when these events needed to be scheduled... He knew the war we would be in.

I woke up on Tuesday, September 11, as a twenty-year-old and everything had changed. I was actually late to work that day (oops), so I had to catch up on what was going on. You could see that Apostle Chuck was in a state of distress because, unfortunately, what God had shown him was now a reality. Even when you have the faith of a giant, you too can be shaken.

We ended up going on with the Future War of the Church conference on the west coast on the 20th of September. We sort of had to press on, considering that we knew we were in the timing of the Lord with the subject matter of the conference. Everything had changed for the country and the world, but it did not change the job of God's people—which was to carry on with the mission we had been given.

This reveals that God is in complete control. He gave a vision to a proven prophet months before the events of September 11, 2001, unfolded. He had a remnant group positioned to intercede, worship, and war at bookended conferences to this horrific event in human history. Even when things look bad and our faith is shaken, God is still in control.

Early 2020 was a very similar point in history—similar to the fall of 2001: Life was comfortable! The economy was humming along, and the future was bright. Then COVID-19 surfaced. But pay attention. God has spoken! He has warned! Anyone who has ears to hear has known the season that we have now entered into was coming. So let me encourage you today: Take heart, because *God has a plan* and He has a people who will be victorious in the battles ahead! Tighten your belts and get ready to do exploits![2]

IN MARCH 2020 DRASTIC SHIFTS BEGAN

By watching Israel and God's people and reaction to them worldwide, we can know times and seasons so we understand God's will in the earth. Since some of my children and grandchildren live in Israel, I regularly stay in touch with what happens there. During this current crisis I have closely watched how the nation of Israel has responded. This has enabled me to know what we should expect here in the United States.

The Lord has ways to order our steps. My son Daniel and his wife, Amber, head up Glory of Zion Jerusalem and have lived in the land for ten years. On March 6, 2020, we received a call from Israel that Amber's father, Jed Sauce, had died unexpectedly. Though things were now happening worldwide at an accelerated rate, Daniel and Amber and their three children had to leave Israel and come to America. International travel was already getting difficult, but the Lord had destined them to be in the United States rather than Israel during the ongoing crisis.

Daniel and Amber have made a significant impact during

their decade living in Israel and are now writing a wonderful book on what they have learned, *Joy in the War*. They have lived through two wars and many dire circumstances in those years. The following account from their new book is so enlightening. Daniel shares:

> The last months of 2019, a strange new respiratory illness began to emerge in Hubei province, China. At first, a small number of cases surfaced in the city of Wuhan with a population of eleven million. The new disease presented with flu-like symptoms, and rapidly progressed into respiratory distress in some patients. This type of illness was familiar to local doctors in the area due to the initial outbreak of SARS in 2002.
>
> After several patients died from apparent cases of viral pneumonia, doctors began to sound the alarm in China. There were early reports of medical personnel and news reporters being threatened by the government and instructed not to spread rumors about the situation.
>
> Reports that a small cluster of novel coronavirus cases had been discovered in Wuhan began to spread through international media around the beginning of January 2020. World powers initially began to downplay the situation as a localized problem while issuing travel advisories for China and other south Asian nations. As sparks thrown from a flame, new cases of COVID-19 began to appear in neighboring countries and predictably along air travel routes.
>
> My wife, Amber, and I were just preparing to travel to Wales in order to minister when news reports of the virus began to dominate the media. We had been looking forward to that trip for a long time, and still

felt that God had covered us to go. While in Wales, we connected with an apostolic center there and were blessed to retrace the steps of the Welsh Revival.

At the same time we were in Wales, three of our team members from Jerusalem had flown to France to go on a ski trip. As we all returned to Jerusalem, one of the young men started to feel ill. The other two showed up to our Sunday meeting. When we found out that one of the young men had stayed at home sick, I asked the other two men to go home until their roommate's condition could be determined.

Within twenty-four hours the news began to report that a cluster of coronavirus cases had been identified in France. After speaking to his doctor, our employee was asked not to come to the hospital as his condition was considered low risk. Another two days passed before the Israeli government released instructions for anyone traveling from France to self-quarantine for 14 days from the date of entry. This meant that all three of our young men had to stay home for another week and a half.

At that point, I called our family doctor who is a close friend and asked him what the situation was in Israel and if we should follow any specific instructions at the ministry center. He reassured me that there were only fifteen cases in Israel and simply limiting meetings to less than a hundred persons was sufficient.

We had also planned a ministry trip to Thailand at the beginning of April and were worried about the potential for our flights being canceled over the virus. Shortly after that, the Israeli media began reporting cases in Thailand and El Al Airlines discontinued service from Israel to Bangkok. We watched as flight after flight was canceled across Asia and some parts of Europe. The list of quarantined countries that Israel mandated grew by the day.

We went to the grocery store and began to stock our freezer and pantry with a month's worth of supplies in anticipation of a possible government-mandated quarantine. At the time, this still felt like a precaution and we were optimistic that the COVID-19 epidemic would slow and fizzle out as spring approached.

Our world really began to change on the night of March 6th when Amber received the call that her father, Jed Sauce, had passed away in Texas. The following day our family had to make a split-second decision to try and travel to Texas to be with family or stay in place at our home in Israel. Feeling at peace over our arrangements, we decided to immediately board a flight for Newark, New Jersey, and on to Dallas, Texas.

As we arrived in Dallas, we almost felt as if someone had hit a rewind button since the United States was just starting to report small clusters of the virus in several states. It seemed that America was at the same point that Israel had been several weeks prior and would follow a similar pattern in transmission and their attempt to contain the spread of COVID-19.

Within forty-eight hours, we started the process all over again of stocking our home with enough food and supplies to last a longer period of time should the government decide to take more drastic measures in the fight against this new enemy. Things began moving very quickly after that as President Donald Trump declared a national state of emergency in a press conference on Friday March 13.[3]

I HAVE NOT GIVEN YOU A SPIRIT OF FEAR

For God has not given us a spirit of fear, but of power and of love and of a sound mind.

—2 Timothy 1:7, NKJV

Daniel continues:

As human beings, we all have something that triggers our deepest, darkest fears. God used these events in my life to show me how He knows what situations will trigger fear, and how to prepare us even from our youth. He knows those things that the devil might use to destroy our faith or slow us down in our pursuit of everything He has called us to.

A spirit of fear itself is our invisible enemy. If you stop and think of most things that cause fear to start taking hold, you will quickly realize that fear of the unknown is at the root of terror. If the devil has a foothold, he will use our own fear responses to create terror.[4]

I (Chuck) want to pause here on this important point, which is highly relevant for the situation we are now in as a church. Is it normal to fear an invisible virus that has killed hundreds of thousands around the globe? Yes. The question therefore becomes, "Lord, how am I to *respond* to this fear?" Again, here is Daniel with a wonderful answer:

Our natural response to fear has to do with the way God designed us, and how we respond to situations that present a hazard. Within God's grace we act to distance ourselves from danger or take actions that remove a potential threat. God designed us with the ability to hear His voice and discern situations that could push us out from under His covering. I love this passage from Psalm 91 as it reminds us that we dwell in the shelter of the Most High and rest in the shadow of the Almighty:

"Whoever dwells in the shelter of the Most High will rest in the shadow of the Almighty. I will say of the LORD, 'He is my refuge and my fortress, my God, in whom I trust.' Surely he will save you from the fowler's snare and from the deadly pestilence. He will cover you with his feathers, and under his wings you will find refuge; his faithfulness will be your shield and rampart. You will not fear the terror of night, nor the arrow that flies by day, nor the pestilence that stalks in the darkness, nor the plague that destroys at midday."

—PSALM 91:1–6, NIV

We will not fear the terror of night nor the pestilence that stalks in darkness. We must allow the Lord to take away our fear of that which exists in darkness. We take our shelter in the presence of the Most High, and the shadow that covers us is not one born of darkness but the shelter of His wings. As I ponder this passage, God also reminds me of the Passover story when the sons of Israel were instructed to take the blood of the sacrificial lamb and place it on the door posts so that death would not visit their first-born. As the Israelites were instructed to take the action of painting the entrances of their homes with blood, God also marked their homes as shelters from the spirit of death that would come by night.

During any crisis we have to ask the Lord how to find our abiding place in Him. We must allow Him to cover us with the grace of His blood. When God speaks, accept the provision of His shelter and allow Him to mark out your boundaries as a refuge. Don't let the devil give you a spirit of fear when there is a provision for your covering.

As time went on, world events continued to test the faith God had given me over my fears of sudden disease outbreaks or the potential use of bio-chemical warfare. I remember watching the news in 1991 as U.S. soldiers in Kuwait and Iraq suited up in full protective gear in anticipation that Saddam Hussein might deploy stockpiles of chemical weapons that Iraq was widely believed to possess. Ironically, those very same weapons would pose an even more direct threat in my life many years later as they had been smuggled across the border into Syria. After moving to Israel in 2011, there was a period of several years when Syria's chemical weapons program was considered a grave threat to Israel.

The world has also seen several concerning disease outbreaks over the last couple of decades. Some of these events include the SARS epidemic of 2002, MERS in 2012, Bubonic Plague in Madagascar in 2017, a sharp global increase in Measles cases in 2019, and the 2013 to 2016 Ebola outbreak that devastated West Africa.

Although I kept up with most of these situations as they occurred, they did not pose any immediate threat to our family or change our routine drastically at the time. Over the years, I almost got used to watching news reports of men dressed in space suits preparing to challenge the next weird tropical disease that was hard to pronounce. After the first SARS epidemic, it became common place to see east Asians wearing paper medical masks as a matter of routine.

This may have seemed like an overreaction at the time, but little did we know this would soon become our own new and rapidly changing reality.[5]

Israel is now leading the nations in innovations, change of perspective, and establishing new boundaries as we combat this invisible enemy.

PASSOVER 2010 PREPARES THE WAY FOR THE FUTURE…ESPECIALLY 2020!

This Passover is key for our future! When I first met Holy Spirit in 1972, I was visited for three days. The Lord revealed Himself to me as the God of Israel. As I learned His Word, there was never a question in my heart about Israel being His firstborn nation. Since 1972 I have carefully observed God's love and discipline for His nation and how Israel continues to reestablish their life and war for their boundaries. I have watched how they war against terrorism and pray that we do the same. I have watched the hatred and acts of violence set against them. I have warred in the Spirit and prayed with them as season after season they establish their political government. However, I have watched God's hand of favor on them also. Because of this, Passover has always been a very key time of "crossing over" into the future.

At Glory of Zion International we have always celebrated Passover, but we knew that Passover 2010 was different. This marked a new decade, and we needed to go public and decree Passover to the church around the world. We had already established a web-based church, so I knew what we did in Denton, Texas (where our ministry was founded), would create ripples around the nation and world. We went *big*! We erected a tent that seated five thousand to celebrate Passover and actually extended our gathering to two weeks like King Hezekiah extended his Passover celebration to two weeks instead of one. We reached 160 nations around the world during that time. Linda Heidler, one of our prophetic scribes, shared the following about that historic time:

> During the conference, we knew that God was doing something extraordinary in reconnecting the blood of the Passover lamb to the crucifixion of Jesus. The church had separated the crucifixion of Jesus from Passover and moved it to the pagan holiday of Easter during the reign of the Roman emperor Constantine. Not since the early Celtic church had the church acknowledged that Jesus was crucified at Passover and raised from the dead on the Feast of Firstfruits.
>
> On January 10, 2010, Chuck prophesied that Passover of that year would realign the church with the power of the blood of Jesus and reconnect the church with the times and seasons God had ordained. God would reestablish what He intended to be observed from generation to generation as an everlasting observance. Leading up to Passover, we had monthly prayer focuses to bring us into corporate revelation of the significance of Passover. Our regular corporate intercession meetings brought additional revelation of God's purposes for Passover and how we were to make prophetic decrees based on them.
>
> During the conference itself, much of what was prophesied was declaring the future of the church for the season we are in today. On April 3, 2010, Chuck prophesied about a season of plowing and being plowed that was preparation for the harvest. He also prophesied about the church coming into a new way

Tribes

of communicating that would allow the voice of nations to be heard.

On March 25, 2010, he prophesied about conflict with world systems aligned with a mammon structure (a pervasive, deceptive spirit aligned with the worship of material wealth rather than God), and conflict along the southern border of the US and Mexico. He prophesied that nations were reaching their crossroads and would have to choose how they would align.

The Passover conference itself was rich in prophetic revelation, but after the conference the revelation continued. On September 24, 2011, Chuck prophesied that since Jesus cleansed the temple at the beginning of His ministry during Passover and cleansed the temple again at the end of His ministry at Passover, we could expect a cleansing of the church at Passover. This would be a direct confrontation of the mammon system.

During the conference, Robert Heidler spoke about Hezekiah and how he cleansed the temple and reinstituted Passover. Israel had not celebrated Passover for many years. They loved it so much that they continued the celebration an additional seven days. Based on this, we continued our Passover celebration beyond the scheduled time for an additional week.

During that time, on April 2, 2010, Cindy Jacobs gave an extensive prophecy to Glory of Zion and the Denton area. Passover 2010 truly set the course for the church for the next ten years. When we celebrated that Passover, reconnecting the blood of the Passover lamb to the blood of Jesus, the ultimate Passover Lamb, it shifted the church.

Before that time, few churches celebrated the true prophetic significance of Passover. Some churches would have a Rabbi come and lead a Passover Seder for their congregation, but this did not really reconnect Passover with the crucifixion. Today there are books, articles, videos, and conferences on the significance of Passover for Christians.[6]

Ten is the number that represents testimony. Just as that conference set the course for the 2010s, Passover of this year is setting the course for the 2020s. God is already saying that these will be years of healing, miracles, and harvest, and it will be wonderful to hear what else He has in store for the years to come. This Passover becomes a testimony.

WATCH ISRAEL!

I will make you a great nation, and I will bless you [abundantly], and make your name great (exalted, distinguished); and you shall be a blessing [a source of great good to others]; and I will bless (do good for, benefit) those who bless you, and I will curse [that is, subject to My wrath and judgment] the one who curses (despises, dishonors, has contempt for) you. And *in you* all the families (nations) of the earth will be blessed. . . . I will greatly bless you, and I will greatly multiply your descendants like the stars of the heavens and like the sand on the seashore; and your seed shall possess the gate of their enemies [as conquerors].

—Genesis 12:2–3; 22:17, emphasis added

He who keeps Israel will neither slumber [briefly] nor sleep [soundly]. The Lord is your keeper; the Lord is your shade on your right hand. The sun will not strike you by day, nor the moon by night. The Lord will protect you from all evil; He will keep your life.

The LORD will guard your going out and your coming
in [everything that you do] from this time forth and
forever.

—PSALM 121:4–8

During this strategic season of "passing over," soften your
heart. Remember Israel. The Lord spoke to Moses for Pharaoh
at Passover and said, "I raised you up for this very purpose, to
display My power in [dealing with] you, and so that My name
would be proclaimed in all the earth" (Rom. 9:17)! Pharaoh hardened his heart over and over. However, after he resisted the Lord,
God hardened Pharaoh's heart. Keep your heart turned toward
the God of Israel. Know His Son. Embrace His Spirit.

CHAPTER 6

The Realignment of Nations

RECENTLY ONE OF my children had been away from the Lord. A couple months ago he rededicated his life and heart back to God. He made quite a statement to me: "Are you telling me I've gotten my life right and now the world's going to come to an end?" And I said, "No, the world is not coming to an end." The Lord showed me shifts that we would make through 2026 in America and throughout the world. The present situation has many economic consequences globally. I discussed that in chapter 4 and will discuss this again.

A NEW ERA IS HERE!

We are in a season of watching! We are watching as captivity is breaking from our promise. Angels are intervening. There is a new commissioning and sending. We are held up in our upper rooms waiting. The time is now to build the future! Last season we were trained to watch, and now we're watching things carefully materialize that were prophesied. The enemy doesn't want to let go of the best of what is yours. You have a portion, and he wants to keep it—that's the law of inheritance. We must recognize that the enemy is trying to capture all the Lord meant for you to enjoy and use for the future.

The crisis that we're in, that the nations are in, hasn't surprised God. One of the things that I have been praying is that this would be the year that the Lord would begin to divide the nations. God has ways of getting us into position for our future. He isn't trying to destroy the world or overly punish us for our mistakes and lack of stewardship. Rather, He desires to position and align us in a new way. He sends rain on the just and the unjust (Matt. 5:45).

EVERYTHING IS CHANGING!

Change can be a very good thing if we communicate it properly. Because immediate changes had to occur because of COVID-19, our minds had not shifted before our actions had to manifest. For schools to close for two months and now through the end of the 2020 school year has caused great stress to enter our homes. This has occurred especially where both parents are in the workplace. I loved reading this from Ben, a young student who had to shift from public school to home school. "It is not going good. My mom's getting stressed out. My mom is really getting confused. We took a break so my mom can figure this stuff out. And I'm telling you it is not going good."[1]

Is this a crisis, or is the Lord restoring family life, especially in America? I have noticed many of us returning to life as it once was in rural America. Growing up, we would sit under trees and talk for hours. We stayed home more. We had a couple of television shows we watched as a family. We ate together and prayed before meals. We played cards and board games.

Had we gotten too far from family life?

The family was God's first war unit; perhaps we were on the verge of becoming defective. Sometimes God uses a very bad situation to cause beneficial things to happen. Of course we grieve over the hundreds of thousands of people who have lost their lives to this current pandemic. But in terms of our key relationships, starting with our time with God and extending to our family and loved ones, the Lord is using this season to interrupt "normal." When our normal becomes consumed with busyness—even good busyness—and emotionally distances us from our key relationships, we can lose connection. So, be conscious of your connections with your family and loved ones.

I encourage you to look at your inner life as well—your intimacy level with the Lord. Yes, things on the outside—the economy, the world, and so on—are in flux and command our attention. However, our spiritual effectiveness in this year and the "pass over" years to come wholly depends on how deeply we are connected with Abba Father. In this season of "girding our belts" to war for God's kingdom, we must stay connected to the Lord in order to accurately hear His voice. As Jesus so lovingly said in John 10:27, "My sheep hear My voice, and I know them, and they follow Me" (NKJV).

Take advantage of whatever time you have during this "interrupted" stage in history to meet with the Father. Press in to hear His voice so that you may activate the watchman anointing!

THERE IS A WAVE OF TURMOIL TOUCHING PLANET EARTH!

Passover is key in the understanding of any Christian's life, as we all are covered and protected by the blood of the Lamb. Dr. Robert Heidler, the incredible teacher I have been connected with for thirty-plus years, has been researching and keeping us abreast of both world news and biblical revelation. He shared several important nuggets with us:

> The last few months we have seen waves of unprecedented disasters sweep the world. In January we saw horrific images of fires sweeping across Australia. Every major city in Australia was surrounded by fire. Some cities were completely cut off—all of the access

roads were blocked by fire. Some in the media called it "Australia's fire apocalypse."

In February 2020 there were reports of unprecedented locust swarms in Africa, the Middle East, and in China. Locusts darkened the skies in Africa, stripped fields bare within minutes, and left famine in their wake. The locusts then moved through the Middle East and ate their way into southern China. Just yesterday (March 31, 2020) I saw a report that locust swarms had moved into Russia. In the Bible, locust swarms are always a sign of God's judgment. Locusts were the eighth plague in Egypt. The whole Book of Joel describes a locust plague as the judgment of God.[2]

Then came the coronavirus. Beginning in one small area of China, now the virus has spread worldwide. At the time of this writing, nations are still in quarantine, businesses are closed, travel is canceled, and the economy is in shambles. One nation that was hit especially hard and is reeling from the effects of the virus is Italy. Of course, Italy's factory infrastructure is owned by China with direct flights from the ground-zero city of Wuhan, China. The Lord is now looking at and adjusting relationships between nations. Travel has slowed to a stop between many nations.

This disruption is almost like a modern-day Tower of Babel confrontation and visitation from heaven to realign earth's communication. In other words, I believe the Lord is "rewiring" the channels, supply chains, and transportation networks that connect nations commercially, economically, politically, and even spiritually. This realignment is necessary as the Lord shifts the world power structures in nations such as China, Russia, and the United States. What will be the long-term effect if, for example,

US companies decide to bring manufacturing home from overseas nations such as China? (More on this in a moment.)

VIRUSES ARE LIKE DEMONS!

Even as far back as 2000, the Lord had me write a whole chapter on plagues in *The Future War of the Church* so we could understand the concept of what's ahead. Viruses are like demons! They must have a host that they can control; they then create fear, immobilize the host, and monopolize time and resources. We create atmospheres in the earth that help them thrive. Specifically, when the power structure of a nation is based on the spirit of mammon (worldly greed and material wealth) rather than the Spirit of God, demons flourish. As societal pillars such as godly leaders; an active, praying church; and biblically based governmental and economic principles are weakened, it gives way for the enemy to wreak havoc. Just like a virus, demonic structures must be attacked at the root and overcome.

One of the key tools the enemy uses virally is fear. Look at our own nation during this crisis, for example. Many people are living in fear. As I mentioned earlier, fear is a natural reaction to stress and crises. But we must stay watchful of fear—are we moving in the Spirit to handle our fear and surrendering it to God, or are we allowing the enemy to infect us with his virus?

During this uncertain time of pandemic, many are asking, "Can this be the judgment of God?" As I mentioned earlier, at the beginning of each January we have a large gathering called Starting the Year Off Right. This gathering helps us focus as we press toward Passover. One key revelation from our January 2020 meeting was that this will be (and is) a year of *visitation*. We usually think of visitation as a time when God's presence and power are manifested in His church. But there's another kind of visitation: when God visits the world with judgment. *Visit* can be the same word as *audit*. Sometimes when Jesus comes, it's not gentle Jesus, meek and mild.

Revelation 19 describes Jesus visiting the world with judgment this way:

> I saw heaven standing open and there before me was a white horse, whose rider is called Faithful and True. With justice he judges and wages war. His eyes are like blazing fire, and on his head are many crowns.... The armies of heaven were following him.... Coming out of his mouth is a sharp sword with which to strike down the nations. "He will rule them with an iron scepter."... On his robe and on his thigh he has this name written: KING OF KINGS AND LORD OF LORDS.
> —REVELATION 19:11–16, NIV

Psalm 2 tells us that the world is in rebellion against God: "The kings of the earth take their stand and the rulers take counsel together against the LORD and against His Anointed" (Ps. 2:2, NASB). The world is always seeking to rebel against God and throw off His moral constraints, and Psalm 2 tells us that for a while, God permits it. He actually finds this puny rebellion amusing, as we're told in Psalm 2:4 (NASB), "He who sits in the heavens laughs." But there comes a time when God stops laughing. The scripture continues, "Then He will speak to them in His anger and terrify them in His fury" (Ps. 2:5, NASB).

There comes a time when God looks down at the world's rebellion and says, "*That's enough!*"

Robert concludes: "I personally believe we have entered into a season of judgment. That does not mean that it's the end of the world. That doesn't mean it's Armageddon! *The conclusion is that the world's rebellion has reached a tipping point, and because of God's love for the human race, He has intervened."*[3]

CONSTANTINE, JUSTINIAN, AND NOW

Many times down through history God has acted in judgment. We have already discussed the Passover when God visited the earth with a whole series of disasters. They were God's way of preparing the world for the miracle of Passover. Robert continued to share with me about God's judgment on the Roman Empire:

> One of the clearest examples of God's judgment in history was the destruction of the Roman Empire. In my book *Messianic Church Arising* I talk a lot about Constantine I.
>
> As Roman emperor, he agreed to end the persecution of Christians, but demanded the church make some changes so it could be more palatable to pagan Romans. At the Council of Nicaea in 325, Constantine made Christianity into a different religion. He outlawed house churches and built magnificent temples for the church to meet in. He changed worship: *Ordinary believers were no longer free to exercise their gifts. Only paid clergy could participate.*
>
> Constantine hated the Jews and wanted to rid the church of anything "Jewish." He replaced the biblical feasts with "Christianized" pagan feasts. Constantine particularly hated Passover. In fact, at the Council of Nicaea, he outlawed it! However, much of the church resisted these changes.
>
> Then, in the sixth century, Justinian became emperor of the Eastern Roman Empire (also called the Byzantine Empire). By this time, the Western Roman Empire had crumbled after centuries of corruption,

greed, and poor leadership. Justinian reigned in his capital of Constantinople from 527–565. His wife, Theodora, was a prostitute who became his mistress, and eventually his empress. Justinian's goal was to restore the Roman Empire to its former greatness. To do that, he set out to unify the church, and he tried to do that by rooting out and destroying what he called "heresy." Heresy included anything that still retained the church's Jewish heritage, especially Passover. Every Passover creates problems!

Justinian's official historian was a man named Procopius. He wrote a history full of glowing praise for his emperor. But Procopius also wrote a "secret history" that he did not allow to be published until after his death. He wanted future generations to know the truth.

In his secret history, he told what Justinian was really like. He described Justinian as a ruthless, evil man. He wrote: "How could anyone put Justinian's ways into words?...nature seemed to have taken the wickedness of all other men combined and planted it in this man's soul....more men [have] been murdered by this single man than in all previous history."[4]

To help unify the church, Justinian declared "heresy" to be an act of treason against the government and tasked his armies with the job of eliminating it. This later provided a legal foundation for the Inquisition and the Crusades! "Heretics" included Jews, and any Christians that celebrated Passover. His persecution of these heretics was brutal! Constantine had outlawed apostolic Christianity, but Justinian eliminated those who practiced it.

Procopius wrote, "In his zeal to gather all men into one Christian doctrine, he recklessly killed all who dissented....Agents were sent everywhere to force whomever they chanced upon to renounce the faith of their fathers....Many were burnt to death at Constantinople. Tortures discovered the heretics, scourging and imprisonment were used to induce them to convert."[5] Justinian sent out armies throughout the empire to root out and destroy the last vestiges of the early church. Whole towns were put to the sword for the crime of celebrating Passover!

God allowed Justinian to continue in his ways for a season, but He finally said: That's enough! The judgment of God fell on Justinian's empire. Historians have noted that Justinian's reign was marked by an unprecedented series of disasters.

- 535—was a "year without a summer." The weather remained cold, the crops failed, and famine struck the empire.

- 541—brought what historians call the "Plague of Justinian." Bubonic plague hit Constantinople and spread across the empire, depopulating entire cities. (The population of Constantinople went from 500,000 to less than 100,000.) It was one of the worst plagues in history.

John of Ephesus, the man who led Justinian's attack on heretics, described the plague this way: "God's wrath turned into...a wine-press and pitilessly trampled and squeezed the inhabitants like fine grapes. Homes, large and small...suddenly became tombs....Ships in the midst of the sea...were suddenly attacked by [God's] wrath and became tombs adrift on the waves."[6]

Then this prophecy came: "Perhaps [during] the remainder of world [history]...they will fear and shake because of the terrible scourge with which we were lashed [because of] our transgressions."[7] John of Ephesus was saying, "We have sinned! This plague is the judgment of God!"

Justinian refused to repent, so more waves of judgment fell:

- 542—An earthquake devastated Constantinople.

- 551—A plague of Anthrax decimated the cattle.

- 557—Another massive earthquake struck and badly damaged the walls of Constantinople.

- 559—Nomadic warriors called the Huns poured into the city through its damaged walls!

- 541–602—The Roman Empire lost one-third of its population, half of its territory, and 70 percent of its revenue.

One writer made this incredible statement: "God, hating the works of this demon emperor, turned his face away!"[8]

Recovery never fully returned. Because of Justinian's ruthless oppression of God's people, God allowed judgment to fall on a nation![9]

A TIME TO THINK TRIUMPH!

In each nation there is a remnant. When a kingdom remnant arises with a strong voice, the atmosphere of heaven enters and spreads through the earth. The Lord does not want us to have a defeatist or fear mentality. Rather, He wants us to triumph! In this year of the voice we must be capable of discerning whether the voices we are hearing are from the Lord or from the enemy to create fear. Do I think the enemy can use this great opportunity to change times and law? *Yes*. But remember, the Lord has a strong people in the earth realm. You are one of those people— one of the watchers! I pray and decree that during this Passover year and season we will fully pass over! God has put a *divine pause* in place until He sees who is willing to cross over with Him through His blood.

NATIONS ARE SHAKING!

In the midst of the viral crisis and its aftermath worldwide, China, Russia, and the United States are still in a tug-of-war vying for world leadership. Another nation that should be watched closely is Korea—North and South together. This is the seventy-fifth year since the nation divided. What will we see as a sign to the world in this nation?

CHINA IS MOVING IN NEW WAYS TO CONTROL TRADE

Like Egypt at the first Passover, manpower and domination of resources are key to recognize. This will be a pattern for the decade ahead—the *pey* decade. I believe at Passover 2020 our eyes have been opened. World trade power is in a chess match. Trade is interesting. Lucifer was cast from heaven because of his iniquity of trading. In other words, Lucifer was looking for ways to gain power through negotiation and dealmaking. He is still doing that today. Fellow watchmen, if we don't understand the warfare over trade systems and how to enforce the kingdom of God, we will never see the transference of wealth for the latter-day harvest. Therefore, to understand Satan's schemes, we must watch trading patterns carefully. *China has ways to pull strings and gain inroads to become the major economic influencer in the world!*

Because we are in an economic war, we will see great conflict between China and America in days ahead. There will be much discussion over who or what truly is the root cause behind this coronavirus.

But the message of this book—and the more critical question of our time—is not in regard to the plague-like invasion of this pandemic. Rather, it is about God realigning power structures both in the earth and in the spirit.

PORTS, CHINA, AND THE ELECTION

On May 6, 2020, as this book was about to go to press, I had a dream that I felt compelled to share.

In the dream I was steering a shipping barge and being used to direct it to its new position in a port. I did a satisfactory job with this first barge that I was helping to dock. (I actually think this first ship represented the ways God led our team to facilitate intercessory prayer efforts within our spheres during President Trump's first term in office.)

However, the timing of the dream then changed. I was now required to dock a second barge in a different port, but this docking job was much trickier and difficult to accomplish. I immediately knew a way to get this barge into port—by the use of mirrors. When I docked the first barge, I had misinterpreted several reflections that had caused me problems. On the mirrors that I was using now, there were key reflections of other nations that were trading in the port. I had to maneuver around and past them to get the boat into position. Once I interpreted what other nations were trading in this new port, I used those dynamics to get the barge positioned.

I had to get the barge through a narrow entryway that was half the size of the barge. I could do this only if I understood how to use the mirrors that were available to me and that I could attach to the barge.

When using mirrors, you see a reversed image, so if you don't interpret the image correctly, your movements are impeded. In my dream there was no way to maneuver the barge successfully through the port to its docking position without the use of mirrors.

I realized that I needed to update my wife, Pam, on my location and what I was doing. I went to use my cell phone to call her but knew it was not the proper way to communicate. It's not that I couldn't use my cell phone—I just knew that by using it, I would thwart the business that we had in the port. In other words, the line was not secure.

By this time, I was in a lounge at the port. I noticed a landline. I unplugged the phone and the line from the wall and brought it into a glass business center setting. I tried to use the landline but couldn't get through and realized I needed a certain code to access an outside line. So I couldn't use the landline to connect with my wife. I knew I could figure out the code but also realized that was not the right mode of communication in this case.

The barge captain came into the lounge and asked if I was trying to use the phone. I said yes. He said, "Using the landline will cost you an exorbitant rate, and you need a code. Let me bring you another device for communication." (I had the impression that someone would trace a landline call to me because of how large the bill would be.)

The captain returned with a new, hidden device. This was an odd pay phone–looking thing about the size of a watch box. I realized that to activate the phone and make a successful connection, a portion of the device had to catch a coin from our current US dollar economy. Once the device was activated, there was a money clip–like wallet/phone that I could use to make my call. This portion of the device, however, required some sort of new currency to activate and operate the device in order to have successful communication.

This currency was like crypto-currency, but it was something else—and I knew I didn't have the proper currency to operate the device and make my connection. Only this new currency could operate the device, and some way or another the currency had a chip in it that would cause the device to work.

And then the dream ended.

Here are some of the things I see in the dream:

- Know that our trade systems will be severely tested! Our trade systems need to get established in current and new ports in the days ahead in new ways. This season of trade ahead will be much more difficult than the last season.

- Realign with key nations. In the dream I saw the reflection of many nations in the mirrors (Spain, Italy, Argentina, Brazil, Mexico, Morocco, Saudi Arabia, Great Britain, and Germany, to name a few). It was those reflections that I was using to maneuver the second barge into the port. These nations had found their way into the port.

- We will contend with China. In my dream I knew China was controlling the overall operations of the

port. As I interpret it, in the days ahead there will be
great contention with China over who will dominate
world trade.

- Our communication system must change as quickly as
  possible. One of China's war tactics (in terms of trade,
  economics, and world power) will be to lock us out
  of certain trade ports. The only way we will be able
  to become established is to maneuver through other
  nations and then communicate using a different type
  of communication system.

- Somehow gold is key in the new currency.

- The president could win a second term. In my dream
  I believe the second port represents the president's
  second term in office. As I write this, I haven't heard
  clearly yet from the Holy Spirit whether the president
  will be reelected and am seeking the Lord daily. But
  this dream was the first inkling in the spirit that I've
  had about a possible second term. As well, and as we
  touched on earlier, the ways in which we operated in
  the last season as a church—and nation—will not
  work in the new season. We must let go of the old. In
  that sense the same is true for the president. For the
  president to be successful in his second term, he must
  understand things that were not interpreted correctly
  in the last season. I know that if Trump doesn't remain
  in office, China will take over as the dominant world
  power in terms of trade and economics.

- Israel is a key. On May 6, Israel's Supreme Court ruled
  that Prime Minister Benjamin Netanyahu could form
  a new government, ending a seventeen-month political

stalemate and preventing the country from plunging into a fourth consecutive election in just over a year. Now we must realign with Israel for trade. When Israel was maturing as a modern nation, many other nations resisted trading and working with Israel. It had to learn creatively how to grow, produce, and use its own food and to develop many other innovative products, devices, and systems. This will be similar for our communication in the future. Israel will help develop ways for us to communicate so our trade system will flourish.

Think of Daniel in exile in Babylon. He moved among—and excelled in—the powerful pagan society that was Babylonia. Daniel worshipped the God of his forefathers and went above the understanding of the Babylonian magicians—much in the same way that Moses was a channel through which God outwitted the sorcerers of Pharaoh. In the Book of Daniel, after Nebuchadnezzar's magicians, astrologers, and sorcerers failed to interpret the king's dream, Daniel was summoned. (See Daniel 2.)

Daniel asked the king to give him time to interpret the dream. Daniel and his companions then sought "mercies from the God of heaven concerning this secret [i.e., the dream], so that Daniel and his companions might not perish with the rest of the wise men of Babylon. Then the secret was revealed to Daniel in a night vision. So Daniel blessed the God of heaven" (Daniel 2:16–19, NKJV).

As we move forward, we must learn from Daniel. As we wait, watch, and follow the Lord's leading on how and when to take action, it is vital that we

- take time to accurately hear from the Lord, just as Daniel did when he asked Nebuchadnezzar for time to seek God (v. 16);

- find like-minded believers who will press in to God as we watch and pray with them in this new season (vv. 17–18);

- have faith that God will meet us in our sphere of assignment and authority and that the *secret will be revealed* to us as the Lord chooses. This might happen through prayer, the Word, other believers, or, as in Daniel's case, a prophetic dream or other prophetic revelation (v. 19); and, most importantly,

- bless the God of heaven for the new revelation and season and for His goodness (v. 19).

We must be like Daniel in the cultural and spiritual Babylon in which we live. He gained such favor with the pagan king that he was even able to save the lives of the magicians. (See Daniel 2:24–25.) He didn't use the magicians' type of access to revelation; he went above it (in the spirit realm) and came back down into it (in the earthly realm). That is exactly what we need to do.

CHAPTER 7

Contending for a New Identity and Freedom

GOD HAS WAYS for His people to survive and eventually thrive in this economic war. The danger for America is not that it will become a Communist country but rather a very materialistic, control-driven nation where the Constitution has limited authority and is preempted by economic resources. This will limit our freedom and liberty. In other words, we must war against the spirit of mammon (unbridled materialistic power and greed) and for God's economy to reign.

The news out of China about how, when, and where the virus actually started has been changing daily—right up to the time we needed to send this book to press. It may take some time to prudently and carefully gather the facts and sift through the rumors, conspiracy theories, and data to get to the actual truth. One thing is certain, however: China has a verifiable history of suppressing news that might tarnish its image or otherwise shine a negative light on its Communist regime. Do you remember the original news stories coming from Beijing in regard to the 1989 Tiananmen Square massacre? Heavy downplay, spin, and denial.

Politico ran a piece recently that put both China and the World Health Organization in the hot seat:

> Without China's deceit and WHO's solicitude for
> Beijing, the outbreak might have been more limited,

115

and the world at the very least would have had more time to react to the virus. China committed unforgivable sins of commission, affirmatively lying about the outbreak and punishing doctors and disappearing journalists who told the truth, whereas the WHO committed sins of omission—it lacked independence and courage at a moment of great consequence.

In effect, China and the WHO worked together to expose the rest of the world to the virus, at the same time they downplayed its dangers.

China acted as you'd expect. Countries that run gulags for religious minorities typically aren't noted for their good governance and transparency. Chernobyl-type cover-ups are what they do. The purpose of the Chinese Communist Party isn't to protect its citizens, let alone the welfare of other countries, but to do whatever seems best-suited to maintain its dictatorial grip on power at any given moment.[1]

What can we learn in the Spirit from the behavior of nations, including China? As we enter this seven-year Passover season, we must watch carefully, pray strategically, and remain attuned to the promptings of the Father.

We must be keen watchers on the wall for our own nation, for certain. As lawlessness rises, even in the US, more laws must be passed to control this spirit throughout the population. The real danger for us is to make economic liaisons and alignments that cause us to look more like China as we proceed into the future. China is not just a Communist nation but a materialistically controlled entity.

China has seemingly bought half the world, including many strategic ports. (See the previous chapter, regarding ports.) To neutralize this goal of the enemy for us as a nation, I took teams to all the port cities in this nation and prayed. I also prayed at many of the port cities worldwide. God's kingdom people have great power in this season to change the atmosphere of cities and nations. However, we must not live with a passive mindset. Rather, we must press in and go to places and speak what God is saying.

God is building a new plan in the earth realm, and this plan includes you. He's drawing His nation of peculiar people out of all nations! We look different. We are "one new man." We are not being driven by race or by gender. Nationalism is not driving us. We are watching what happens in nations without getting entangled in the political world system. We are standing and changing nations from our heavenly place of authority as we stand in intercession.

Political conflict and tension will be greater than we have ever known.

My son Daniel Pierce had a recurring dream that he communicated to me:

> I was in a camp leading an army. We were positioned on top of a mountain. We were staying in old-style canvas tents. It was night, and I recall looking up at the moon, which was shining through a tree. The tree was one that you would see in Asian pictures and carvings. I moved to the edge of a cliff, with my army standing behind me. Below in the valley was an encampment of enemy soldiers. I knew I was viewing into the Chinese army. There were far more of them than there were of us. However, I had a sense of peace. I knew the army backing me could defeat them. I also knew that we could not move forward until the dawn broke forth!

We can defeat this spirit of invasion of capitalistic control if we move correctly as God's people. A new day is breaking in the church. Harvest angels are being sent to back the army of the Lord and His covenant people. China will be the nation of dichotomy. It will have an army set against the purposes of God and His people.

At the same time, however, China will send forth the greatest army of harvesters the world has ever known. According to a 2018 report by the Council for Foreign Relations:

> China has witnessed a religious revival over the past four decades, in particular with a significant increase in Christian believers. The number of Chinese Protestants has grown by an average of 10 percent annually since 1979. By some estimates, China is on track to have the world's largest population of Christians by 2030.[2]

Think about that startling statistic: the nation that is striving to become the dominant economic power in the world is also seeing an explosion of growth as the persecuted church there continues to thrive. That is true dichotomy!

A VISION OF CHINA

In 1986 I received a vision in which the Lord revealed to me what would happen in the next forty years in ten-year increments. Much of what He showed me revolved around the church and a change in His kingdom development. However, the nation with its leadership and people that He used as an example was China. Here are the details from my vision that involved China.

- 1986—This would be the turning-point year for China. The government of the land would arise, and from its oppression much change would begin to occur in the people. The church in China had always been very oppressed and controlled by the government. I had developed a great relationship with the five key leaders of the massive underground church. This was the year of student revolutions forming to resist the oppression of the government.

- 1989—The Tiananmen Square protests took place, resulting in a massacre that awakened the world to China.

- 1996—The government of the nation began to appear to be more open to the world. I knew immediately the government of the church had to arise in a new way. An apostolic awareness would enter the earth, and new leadership across the earth would arise with a mind for a change from the last church structures to a new kingdom movement. This was the year Peter Wagner convened the National Symposium on the Postdenominational Church at Fuller Seminary. Bishop Bill Hamon regards it as the historical turning point for public recognition of the new apostolic move- ment. The church in China, with incredible leadership, would become an integral part of this move. Since that time, this move has swept the world.

- 2006—China would come into the world picture. This would be the year China would take its rightful place as a national power worldwide.

- 2008—The World Olympics were held in Beijing. No one could have even imagined this twenty years prior.

- 2016—By Rosh Hashanah 2016 (September/October), China would vie to establish its identity as the most influential nation in the world economy. It would plan a developmental strategy for its economy to be second to none. At this point the United States would realign itself with China, and they would become allies. This would become a danger. Conflict would arise, and the two nations would begin to separate their alliance by 2018.

- 2020—China would make the greatest move to gain world economic authority. It would attempt to bring nations under subjection to its dominant economy—by any means. Therefore, when COVID-19 began making headlines in 2019 from its fifth-largest city, Wuhan, I knew the time was now to watch China. This is what caused me to know that this would be not just a virus that would affect China but something that would sweep the globe. I also knew that this virus would become a pawn in a world economic chess match.

- 2026—The goal of national China is to be the most dominant controlling economic force in the world by 2026.

WE NEED A HEALER!

There are times when God stops us from moving and causes us to pause. Why? *Because we need a Healer!* The current issue is not just about a plague or the coronavirus. The real issue is that God is *pausing* us to rearrange the order of our lives. Because of that, we need a Healer! But if we choose to move forward when God is saying to be still, we give the enemy the ability to work. If we pause, the Healer will triumph. The Healer will reveal what you need and how to walk in this pause.

Remember that watchers often stay in one place for a significant amount of time. Think of the job of a military sentry, today or five thousand years ago in ancient Israel. In both cases—and down through history—a sentry's job is to stand and watch. The Lord told the prophet Ezekiel, "Son of man, I have made you a watchman for the people of Israel; so hear the word I speak and give them warning from me" (Ezek. 3:17, NIV).

So, there is a time to watch in the Spirit, and there is a time to move. But we must wait for the Lord and seek His timing. Once we are in His timing, the glory becomes our rear guard. In other words, as we walk in the confidence and favor of God's planning and purpose, His glory, favor, and anointing undergird and strengthen us. Then we have the authority to tell the enemy not to put his hands within our boundaries.

Biblically the only time I see that the enemy has a right to get a hand or a toehold in our boundaries is through three dynamics: *unforgiveness, anger, and greed.* If we operate in unforgiveness and anger, the enemy can get an upper hand in our lives and in our belongings. Once we are filled with forgiveness, all the schemes of the enemy break. (See 2 Corinthians 2:10–11.)

Since 1996 the church has been in a season of maturing apostolically. Now we are being commissioned and sent again. We need to be willing to unlock the glory of God in every place our feet step. Wherever God sends you, cross over with a mind to build for the future.

Let me summarize this new era. This *divine pause* is allowing for God's house to be rebuilt. This era is about the voice that comes out of your house! A supernatural, mystical atmosphere is contending for authority. You determine the rules in your boundaries and sphere. The words coming out of your house are important. If faith isn't coming out of your house, step back, *wait a minute, regroup, and speak again.*

Do not be afraid to perceive the supernatural, mystical season. We must know by the Spirit how to fight our battles. For the

Lord tells us that it's "not by might, nor by power, but by my spirit, saith the LORD of hosts" (Zech. 4:6, KJV). That is how you're going to win these wars ahead. There is a war over authority. This war can be heard, seen, and perceived in the spirit in almost every dimension of society. The enemy is trying to negate God's authority and prevent Him from having a clear voice.

Let your voice be heard!

HE SENT HIS WORD TO HEAL US

Psalm 107:20 is very key in this new era of warfare that we're entering. I believe this era is a true Passover era. The entire ten years, we must pass over and keep passing over. We'll have to deal with things in the nations that we've never dealt with before. *"He sent His word and healed them, and rescued them from their destruction"* (emphasis added). We must have His Word penetrate us to heal us! His Word brings us life and makes us whole. His Word transports us to a place where destruction cannot overtake us.

We are completing one major season in our time and entering another. *Do not back up!* With so much change going on around us, we still want to keep moving. Without faith it's impossible to please God, and what is not of faith is sin. When we violate faith, we have to reconcile our being with the Lord and come back into a new place of wholeness. It is very important to exercise faith in the midst of crisis. If you don't exhibit faith, then you have to ask for forgiveness and restore your relationship with the Lord.

The enemy wants to negate our faith! The thief comes only to steal, kill, and destroy what you were meant to enjoy! Just believing in the Lord is not a threat to the enemy if your faith is negated or neutralized. Demons believe in the Lord. Unless people around you see your faith demonstrated, they will not be attracted to the object of your faith: Jesus. Therefore, we must have a steady stream of faith coming out of our mouths in days ahead. Faith cometh!

A HEALER CAME!

After Israel passed over, they did not get very far before God had to intervene. Look at Exodus 15 when the Healer came. *Why did He come?* He came because the children of Israel had come out from under all these plagues. They had watched the Lord miraculously open the way for their escape as the Red Sea parted. However, after three days of journey they started complaining and murmuring over their future.

Stop now and decree that complaining and murmuring over your future will not be released from the inner recesses of your heart. We have a good future!

The Israelites were only thirty miles from where they started, and they became thirsty. The only water they could find was bitter. Instead of crying out to the Lord again, they complained. The Word of God says the Lord made a statute and ordinance for them, and there He tested them and showed them a tree that could make the water sweet. (See Exodus 15:22–27.)

This was a precursor to the cross of Jesus. This is also a demonstration of exploits and the use of resources. There is always something around you for you to use at your point of need. The Lord came down! He admonished them that if they would obey Him and listen to His commandments and keep them foremost in their thoughts, He would not put on them any of the diseases that He put on the Egyptians. He said, "For I am the Lord who heals you" (Exod. 15:26, nkjv). What He was really saying is, "You need a Healer, and I have come down to be that on your behalf."

We need a Healer in our current Passover season and decade.

You will not get very far in your future without a Healer. The Healer is here to bring you to the expected end that God has for you. Jehovah Rapha came down to earth; if we know the Lord Jesus Christ, *He is now embodied inside our lives.*

He came to earth to reveal what you need so you can walk in healing. If you need Benadryl, He'll show it to you. If it's ipecac, He will show it to you. If it's Tylenol, He will show it to you. He will reveal what you need to make the life source in you flow correctly. Don't tell people they can't take an aspirin. If you need an aspirin, God will show you aspirin. You can take anything God shows you to take, because what He is revealing to you is for your healing. If God shows you chemotherapy, take the treatments. He might not want some of you to take anything—but we can't lean on our own understanding. The Healer has come to reveal our healing. He is the Great Physician and can send you to an earthly physician to help you. However, He is the Healer and can also reveal Himself to you as the One who heals miraculously!

He can pause our movement toward greediness and rebellion! (See Numbers 11–12.) Fragrant prayer offerings can stop plagues! (See Numbers 16.) Idolatry and sin are like the venom of a deadly snake. A greater sacrifice, greater than the bite of a serpent, can neutralize poison! (See Numbers 21.) The Lord reminded us that when we gather, we should remember Him—the power of Communion! (See Matthew 26:26–28, Luke 22:19–20, and 1 Corinthians 11:23–25.) We live in a fallen world, and the enemy will take any opportunity to use that fallenness to create disease and try to take us all out. He comes to kill, steal, and destroy, so we've got to be wise in this thing.

Break out of religion, fast, and take shabbat! Your healing can break forth! Isaiah 58:13–14 says, "If you turn back your foot from [unnecessary travel on] the Sabbath, from doing your own pleasure on My holy day…and honor it, not going your own way or engaging in your own pleasure…I will make you ride on the high places of the earth." The Lord will restore air travel eventually, but it will change drastically.

Here are a few things I am suggesting we all do in this season of allowing the Lord to reset our time and boundaries:

1. Find a shabbat in your life. The Lord requires a shabbat from us to break the cycle of life that we have been in. By Friday night, rest in some way so that you are restored. Many times while ministering in Las Vegas, I have shared that the Lord would require a shabbat in that city that never slept. With the closing of casinos in that city, it finally happened. God requires a shabbat if we are going to walk in health and healing. No one understands this better than I, as I have violated shabbat at certain times in my life.

2. Give an offering. The Lord honors and remembers when you give a portion of yourself to Him. You always want to give to someone more legitimate than yourself.

3. Take Communion. Always remember the power of Yeshua's broken body and shed blood.

4. Fast one day this week. Hear the Lord on how and when to fast this week.

We need a Healer. Father, we ask You to please heal this land. Please heal the nations that cry out for You. We ask You to set a bloodline over every person who is listening, every person who will listen and claim the blood of the Lord Yeshua of Nazareth, so that

the enemy cannot penetrate. Lord, make us cautious.
Make us aware.

WILL THERE BE A NEW NORMAL AFTER WE PASS OVER IN 2020?

Let me reiterate that I believe this whole decade will become a Passover decade. I travel worldwide, and much of my life involves speaking, sometimes to large groups in various nations. However, Pam, my wife, and I disciple several young men and women that the Lord has brought into our lives. These young men and women are on the go in many areas of life. Most have children who are very busy and involved in many activities in both school and their communities. So, after three months of limited activity, quarantine, and accomplishing creative projects, I asked them how things will change in their lives once this pandemic passes:

- Know what is truly important in life. Reevaluate your life goals more frequently. In your new normal this is a great opportunity to get rid of anything that you don't want to hold on to as you cross over. I see many relationships and time-consuming activities falling by the wayside.

- Understand how to stay in the Spirit's perfect timing. When He says go—go! When He says leave—leave! Learn to walk in and by the Spirit.

- Bring our emotions under subjection to the Spirit of God. Fear should never control our actions. Fear is an emotion and also a spirit. We must not allow the spirit of fear to access our normal emotion of fear. Pray for the Holy Spirit to help you discern the difference, and He surely will.

- Find and understand the gifts of the team with whom you are meant to be associated. Teamwork is key. When the Lord ascended, He gave gifts that were necessary in the earth to bring us into a faith explosion. When gifts align properly, we break into new, overcoming power. This is what will accomplish our mission.

- There are many patterns in the Word and in the operation of the world around us. We must stay alert to key patterns so we can know how to react offensively at a certain moment. Moments create events. The Lord told us that we should be more shrewd than the sons of Belial—to be discerning toward the people of the world. (See Luke 16:8–10.)

- Do not grow passive in decreeing your portion. Many people have a "que sera, sera" attitude: if the Lord wants something to happen, then He will just see that a breakthrough is accomplished. The Lord will not do anything that you are supposed to do. Many people never place a demand on the portion that they should have. Some settle for one portion when the Lord would give them ten, thirty, sixty, or even one hundred. Don't settle for less!

- Failure should be looked at as training. Anger should not be a manifestation of imperfection.

The financial crisis ahead could frighten many people. However, God is our Creator and Provider. Let's watch Him do a great work in us for such a time as this. Much of the time, we live on the defensive. Let's watch the signs and learn to react more proactively.

WE MUST PROPHESY

We must speak forth our future. Without prophecy, we lose vision. Without boundaries, we lose vision. We are still having essential staff attend services at Global Spheres Center. On March 29, Daniel Pierce began to prophesy about this Passover from Exodus 12.

> Now you are to eat it in this manner: [be prepared for a journey] *with your loins girded* [that is, with the outer garment tucked into the band], your sandals on your feet, and your staff in your hand; you shall eat it quickly—it is the Lord's Passover. For I [the Lord] will pass through the land of Egypt on this night, and will strike down all the firstborn in the land of Egypt, both man and animal; against all the gods of Egypt I will execute judgments [exhibiting their worthlessness]. I am the Lord.
>
> —Exodus 12:11–12, emphasis added

Daniel went on to say,

> A Passover principle is to simplify and tighten your belt. Tightening your belt symbolizes preparing for what's to come. The Lord is opening a great movement before us. Speak to the mountain that is going to have to move and picture the Lord "tightening His belt around us this Passover as we move forward." The Lord told the people to clean out, simplify, and get ready to move quickly.

WE MUST BE A PEOPLE FILLED WITH IMAGINATION— LIKE EARLY PIONEERS OF NATIONS

Isaiah 26 is wonderful in The Passion Translation. I love the way verse 3 is phrased: "whose imaginations are consumed with you" (Isa. 26:3, TPT). The Hebrew word translated "imagination" is *yester*, meaning "form, concept, framework, imagination, mind." A human imagination, wholly owned by Holy Spirit, is one of the most powerful redemptive forces on earth. These times call for a critical, God-filled imagination. This will create a new framework and conceptualization of all the problems around us. Our minds should be fixed on Him and become consumed by Him. This is what will unleash the supernatural creativity resident in all of the redeemed and give birth to the exploits necessary for our triumph. In this season we must reform our minds and imaginations. We must gather raw materials, then shape them into form and identify our future. Our concepts, frameworks, minds, and imaginations must unlock into new forms and identities to meet and triumph in the era ahead.

Lisa Lyons, who assists Brian Kooiman and me on a day-to-day basis, is a wonderful prophetess. She shares:

> Many years ago, I had a dream in which I was walking around the outside of a house that had incredible architectural detail on every single part of it, woodwork and masonry, from the largest structural features to the smallest minute trim work. I was awed and overwhelmed at the intricate creativity that was evidenced in the house, and in the dream I thought to myself, "I could never imagine all these wonderful things if I was awake." Well, the time has come to do just that...to dream with our eyes wide open. *We must wake up and*

*believe that we can go beyond our present limitations
and into a new, miraculous dimension!*[3]

ONLY A NEW MOVE OF GOD WILL STOP THE OPPRESSION IN THE EARTH

"Behold, the days are coming," says the LORD, "when
the plowman shall overtake the reaper, and the treader
of grapes him who sows seed; the mountains shall drip
with sweet wine, and all the hills shall flow with it."

—AMOS 9:13, NKJV

We are approaching a presidential election in the United
States. One of the words for *visitation* is linked with how you
cast a vote. How we vote is how we will get visited as a nation
in our future. Dutch Sheets and I recently covered America on
a twenty-two-region, twenty-five-city journey. The triumphant
remnant has made incredible headway in the last four years.
Our goal was to awaken the seeds of revival that have been
sown throughout America.

We were also directed to encourage an incredible triumphant remnant to keep advancing. Cry out for a visitation of
His Spirit. His Spirit needs to baptize and cleanse mankind so
that as we walk in the earth, the land rejoices. We must renew
our relationship and covenant with a *holy God* through *His Son*
and by *His Spirit*!

A TIME TO PLOW

Prophetic seeds that have been sown and declared in your region
should be plowed up! The Lord has put us into a plowing season.
The prophetic seeds that didn't come up in one season should be
declared alive and receive a new breath of His Spirit. I see teams of
plowmen being connected together. Many of us have received revelation but tried to plow alone. However, if we connect and plow

together, the harvest of God in a region will be gathered. This is a key time for alignment. We must not lose any momentum of righteous change that has influenced our nation over these last several years.

I prophesied that "I see the enemy throwing some 'dark horses' into this next season." Dark horses are those things that will try to preempt God's plan and end up taking prizes that belong to His people. We must stay focused as watchman intercessors. We must be aware of the enemy's plans to insert circumstances as well as people in an attempt to stop what the Spirit of God is desiring to do now.

In August 2019 I started hearing what the Lord was saying for this new era of Passover ahead. To help you better prepare for this new season, I want to suggest four key books:

- *The New Era of Glory* by Tim Sheets
- *Watchman Prayer* by Dutch Sheets
- *A Triumphant Kingdom* by Robert Heidler and me
- *Time to Defeat the Devil*, a book I wrote for Charisma House

We are entering a new era in which we are crossing over into revelation. These books will help establish you as you advance. End old cycles and enter into what He is announcing for your future.

A NATION RESPONDING

I see this nation responding to Him. I see other nations responding to Him as well. I see nations that aren't responding having tremendous problems. You have to look at statistics. We've had terrible, plague-like conditions before. When you look at this viral infection that is changing the course of the world, there is an unknown factor that we must take into account. This is causing anxiety and a fear of the future to grip many. The major overhaul of the government of the nations of the earth is causing us to reevaluate our priorities and relationships.

GOD IS CHANGING US!

How we minister is changing. For those of us who have traveled and communicated worldwide, we are experiencing a true shift in how we advance.

We have had so many heated demonstrations over the borders of nations. However, this invisible enemy has caused many borders to be secured in supernatural ways. This is no longer just a border war between Mexico and America, Syria and Lebanon and Israel; now even borders between states like Louisiana and Texas are being monitored. Cities are also being monitored in new ways. We must watch carefully our comings and goings.

This pause is a good time to make the Passover changes we have discussed in these chapters. Remove items and structures you no longer need. We must be more cautious about how we gather. Free meetings have shifted. We must ask, "Why do we need to gather and meet in person?"

We must be more cautious about how we operate in finance and be on guard about greed. I think greed and lust for power are the greatest of all the problems in nations today. We must become more compassionate and gain a better understanding of people's needs throughout the world instead of seeing things solely through the lens of rich versus poor.

Many have lost sight of the reality of the world around us. We must start seeing the world—and how people have been affected by crises—through the compassionate eyes of Jesus. Have we become calloused to the struggles of those in our spheres, neighborhoods, cities, and nations? The Lord is making us feel for the people who are experiencing hardships in the world around us.

IS THIS VIRUS EVIL? IS GOD ALLOWING THIS? IS GOD *DOING* THIS?

Viruses and sickness are evil! But God! Those who love Him are having their lives and purposes developed within them even in the midst of evil. This is my wife's favorite scripture: "See then that you walk circumspectly, not as fools but as wise, redeeming the time, because the days are evil" (Eph. 5:15–16, NKJV). If you are interested in this concept of stewarding your time well—redeeming the time—then I recommend my book *Redeeming the Time*.

We have to understand that we live in a fallen world. Man creates many iniquitous pits that we can fallen deeper into. But God always has a plan—plan A, plan B, plan C, plan D—He never runs out of plans of redemption because of His love for mankind! If we listen, the Spirit of God will maneuver us through the time in which we live. He speaks to us and gives us wisdom and revelation. And He says, "If you'll do this one thing, I will respond to you! This hardship is hard but not complicated. All you have to do is listen and obey, and I'll walk your way through this."

The Lord is rearranging how we see disease and sickness. I consider that we have done things that have allowed disease to enter our atmospheres. Yes, the Lord died for mankind and broke the headship of the evil adversary in the earth realm. However, he left man to enforce what He had shed His blood for. Passover should be a daily celebration in our lives, but we don't always enforce what the Lord wants us to enforce.

I think God always has plans for us, for our betterment. However, we must exercise the same power that resurrected Him from the dead over death, hell, and the grave! If we don't enforce what He would have us enforce in the earth realm, the whole earth suffers. Lands are crying for healing! Yes, we still need a Healer to come!

THE KINGDOM OF GOD IS ARISING!

There is a new move of God in His people in this hour! They are like a river of glory fire—liquid gold flowing throughout lands. They resemble fiery lava moving from state to state, province to province, and nation to nation throughout the earth. These glory warriors will destroy the works of the enemy in days ahead. Over the next several years—through this *pey* decade—we will mature into a people who do exploits and are ready to go to war against any darkness attempting to bring destruction to our Lord's kingdom plan.

These triumphant people are ones who know how to triumph. To *triumph* is to obtain victory, or a state of being victorious in conquest. Triumph carries a distinct emotion for God's children; in triumph, one expresses joy or exultation because he or she has prospered, succeeded, and flourished. To triumph means to celebrate and rejoice with victory and jubilation. Triumph indicates that an advantage has been gained over the enemy. Triumph also conveys that success has been granted through a supernatural grace being released.

God has a people who must keep moving in the earth. Movement is linked with life! If we stop moving, we stagnate or routinize. If there is one thing I have seen happen from season to season, it is that the church stagnates. Sometimes this is because we fall into apathy; however, most times we stagnate because we enjoy getting comfortable in one season and resist change. We must be a people who are willing to war for our future.

APOSTOLIC/PROPHETIC RULE MUST BE ESTABLISHED IN A NEW WAY

As the apostolic church matures and advances the kingdom of God in the earth, apostolic/prophetic rule will be established in territories. *Know your field and sphere.* Faith works in place and time. In 2 Corinthians 10 Paul talks about fields, or spheres. We all have key fields and spheres within which we can war and triumph and where we *mobilize the armies.* Know who is warring with you for the King's rule. Press in as you do the following:

- Strategically know your redemptive "thin" places. When Rose Sambrook from Northern Ireland came to speak at one of our gatherings, she shared how in Ireland they talk about "thin places." These are the places where the Spirit of God has come and heaven and earth have become very close. These places have key altars that need to be refired for today. We must know where these altars are in our field or spheres. If there are no thin places in our sphere, then we must find where the Lord wants to come and create a thin place, or a portal between heaven and earth.

- Sanctify the land. When we commit iniquitous sins and defile the land, we must sanctify the land. The land mourns until we have reconciled it back to God, the One who made it. "The earth is the LORD's, and the fulness thereof" (Ps. 24:1, KJV).

- Define the high places. Within our spheres and field we also have high places. These are places where the enemy has erected his rule. These are the places contending for our worship.

- Declare that high places and ruling demonic centers must fall! The enemy has erected many high places throughout the nations. These are the result of the worship war going on in each territory of the earth. Worship occurs around the one whose throne has been established. We are created to worship; if we pay homage to the enemy, he controls the atmosphere. The entire territory then falls under the darkness of his presence, and demonic hosts redirect those in that territory away from God's plan of fullness, peace, joy, and abundance.

- Build a new glory altar. Throughout the Word of God new altars had to be built. How do we do this? We must find the places where religion and government have met and made wrong choices and must bind the strongman. (See Matthew 12.) We must overthrow the defilement of the last altar. (See 2 Chronicles 34:4, John 2:14–15, and Revelation 2:13.) We must contend for His name to be established within us so "all the peoples of the earth will see that [we] are called by the name of the LORD" (Deut. 28:10, NASB). We must let worship ascend and watch His glory come down. (See John 4; Acts 4–11.) We must welcome a new move of His Spirit (Acts–Ephesians).[4] I want to suggest that you read the new book that Robert Heidler and I have just completed, *A Triumphant Kingdom: The Apostolic Church Advancing*. This book will help you move into your future.

A SEVEN-YEAR WINDOW FOR DIVINE HARVEST STRATEGIES

When judgment comes, we must receive mercy, walk in FAITH, and share the good news with all of those around us in a world of chaos! Times of distress are opportunities for miracles. Walk in faith, choose to praise God, and cry out for mercy! People are longing to hear good news. This is our time to pray that people turn and find the Healer in the midst of chaos. Judgment comes so healing can abound, restoration can occur, and our latter may be greater than our former.

THE TIME OF HARVEST IS NOW!

Biblically, God's goal for us is the harvest. We see this all the way through the Bible. God wants our barns to be filled with plenty and our vats to overflow. He wants us to experience the fullness of His promised blessings. That's what harvest means. Harvest is what we've been working and praying for and the promise that we have been pressing forward to attain. The time will come when we will receive the harvest. Harvest is not "pie in the sky, by and by" but the reality of the promise coming into our experience.

God wants us not only to harvest in the natural realm but also to see a harvest of righteousness. He wants us to experience a harvest of souls. Psalm 1 tells us that God wants each of us to be like a flourishing tree that brings forth its fruit in its season. Ecclesiastes 3 tells us there is a time and a season for everything. There is a time to plant seeds, and there is also a time to reap the harvest.

The Bible is written around harvest cycles. The Lord wants His people to develop and maintain a harvest mentality. He wants us to walk in a mindset of increase and reaping. This is an era when we must decree that what we have sown will come forth and multiply. Call back the bread that you have cast upon the waters. The seeds that have fallen in the earth are ready to break forth into an abundant crop. Plow up your fallow ground. Unlock what has never manifested in your past. Let your sorrows turn to joy. Gain new strength! Rise up and enter this era with a mind to triumph!

KNOW HIM!

The Book of Romans says:

> But that's not all! Even in times of trouble we have a joyful confidence, knowing that our pressures will develop in us patient endurance. And patient endurance will refine our character, and proven character leads us back to hope. And this hope is not a disappointing fantasy, because we can now experience the endless love of God cascading into our hearts through the Holy Spirit who lives in us!
>
> —Romans 5:3–5, tpt

Janice Swinney, our senior pastor at Global Spheres Center, shared this with me recently. It is symbolic of the season we are walking into as a church:

> I was driving south toward the Global Spheres Center. The weather was overcast with sprinkles of rain— not enough for my windshield wipers, though. One moment I could see perfectly, and the next moment every window in my car was covered with thick fog. I released a cry: "Jesus, help me!" I was blind to everything outside my car. At that moment, I hit my windshield wipers, and vision returned. As I looked at the cars around me, not all of them had the fog on their windows, but many did. Panic was ensuing. It took

several minutes—possibly two miles—before the windows of my car cleared. When I finally got to the Center, I began praising and thanking God for His great protection.

Many are confused and in a fog at this time in history. Cry out to the Lord! The Lord is real! In the midst of the crisis around you, I pray you know *Him*—the power of His resurrection and the sweetness of His grace and the wholeness of His peace. If you are not sensing His love, stop! Be still. Submit your heart and the plan for your life to Him. Talk to Him as if you and I are sitting together. Let Him know your heart. Roll your cares upon Him. Let all anxieties be turned into praise. Reach your hand and feel His hand. He is there!

IS WAR AHEAD A REALITY?

Let your yea be yea, and nay be nay. (See Matthew 5:37, KJV.) A definite yes: war is ahead! We have seen from this COVID-19 pandemic that we are in a new type of warfare. We must learn to establish bloodlines. We must take up the mantle of this Passover season and walk under the blood of the Lamb as we cross over treacherous and unknown ground.

If you will remember from the beginning of the book, my family always tried to make sure that my imagination was in full alignment with reality. And this is reality, dear ones: God is real. I am so thankful that He visited with me during this period beginning in late August 2019 so we were not caught off guard by the current happenings worldwide. I hope this writing helps you tremendously. Let me conclude by saying one thing: We must ready ourselves for war—both spiritual and physical. We must ascend in worship. We must learn to set the blood of Yeshua of Nazareth as a boundary over our boundaries.

I decree that we are entering into a time of walking victoriously by His Spirt throughout the earth. We will be known because of His Spirit living in us, and our faith will work by His love that we demonstrate to the world around us.

Fellow watchers and warriors, I want to end this book with a word to release the anointing of God's Spirit. Be encouraged by the Lord:

> *This is a day that I am visiting My people. This will be a decade when I align the hosts of heaven with the armies of earth. You are entering a season to walk in an Issachar anointing. In your "process of time," you are ending and beginning. I am declaring that you will end seasons strong and begin new seasons stronger.*
>
> *I am aligning heaven's gates with earth's gates. I am declaring you will be at the right place at the right time. My word is coming alive in a new way. Receive the spirit of revelation and an anointing to interpret every step you take in the days ahead. There is a great war between death and life in the earth realm. Stay one step ahead of death! Watch carefully, for I am unfolding and revealing dimensions of time that have been closed in past seasons.*
>
> *I am creating a winning team in the earth! Many of you signed up for My team, but you didn't want the discipline to become what I needed in the last hour of history. However, in this hour of history, I will draw you forth. Do not despise My disciplines. I am creating a winning team that will know how to pass the ball, work together, and triumph in the end. This is the beginning of a triumphant movement throughout the*

earth, and I say, "My team will win!" The power of Satan's accusing, condemning, and confining strategies will be overcome by this triumphant people.

Your promises are beginning to manifest around you. New levels of prophecy for your future are starting to bud in your atmosphere. Remove any past judgment that has caused you to hold captive your future. I am releasing a new grace of prophecy upon My people. Know that your times are in My hands. The anointing breaks the yoke. Let Me anoint you new and fresh for the era ahead!

The Timetable of Passover

T HE TIMETABLE OF Jesus' crucifixion when compared with the Passover celebration is just incredible. According to the Torah, at the time of Passover a number of events had to take place in a specific order and at specific times.[1]

1. THE PASSOVER LAMB HAD TO BE SELECTED ON A SPECIFIC DAY.

Exodus 12 instructs that the Passover lamb be chosen *on the tenth day of the first month.* By the time of Jesus, only lambs from Bethlehem were considered eligible to serve as Passover lambs. So the lamb born in Bethlehem was chosen and brought into Jerusalem from the east (down the Mount of Olives) and entered the city through the sheep gate.

On the tenth day of the first month Jesus, the Lamb born in Bethlehem, came down the Mount of Olives and entered Jerusalem. (This is called His "triumphal entry"!) As He entered, the people waved palm branches and shouted, "Blessed is He that comes in the name of the Lord! Save us, son of David!" (Matt. 21:9, my paraphrase). By mass acclamation Jesus was designated Israel's Messiah! The crowds had chosen their Passover Lamb.

2. THE LAMB THEN HAD TO BE EXAMINED.

The Torah instructed that once the lamb was chosen, it had to be carefully examined for blemishes. Only a perfect, spotless, unblemished lamb would suffice for the Passover.

After arriving in Jerusalem, Jesus went to the temple to teach. While there, He was approached by the Pharisees, Sadducees, Herodians, and teachers of the Law. Each group posed difficult questions, trying to trap Him. (See Luke 19:47–48.) Essentially, they were looking for any blemish that might disqualify Him as Messiah. But no one could find fault with Him. He was without blemish.

3. THE LEAVEN (IMPURITY) MUST BE CAST OUT.

The Torah instructs that before the feast, all leaven (impurity) must be cast out of every Israelite home. Each mother took a candle and searched out impurity, removing it from her house. This regulation is still observed today. Passover is a time to cleanse every house. Every observant Jewish family carefully cleans their house before Passover. Every trace of impurity is removed.

After Jesus arrived in Jerusalem, He entered the temple and cast out the moneychangers (Matt. 21:12–13). He was following the biblical instruction to prepare for Passover by cleansing His Father's house.

4. THE LAMB WAS TAKEN TO THE ALTAR FOR PUBLIC DISPLAY.

On the morning of *the fourteenth day of the first month,* when all has been set in order, the lamb is led out to the altar. *At 9:00 a.m.,* the lamb is bound to the altar and put on public display for all to see!

On the morning of *the fourteenth day of the first month*, when all had been fulfilled, Jesus was led out to Calvary. *At 9:00 a.m.,* just as the lamb was being bound to the altar, Jesus was nailed to the cross and put on public display at Calvary!

5. THE LAMB WAS SLAIN AT A SPECIFIC TIME.

At exactly *3:00 p.m.* the high priest ascended the altar. As another priest blew a shofar on the temple wall, the high priest cut the throat of the sacrificial lamb and declared, "It is finished!" At *3:00 p.m.* on that High Holy Day, at the moment the Passover lamb was being killed, Jesus cried with a loud voice, "It is finished," and gave up His Spirit! In Greek the term translated "It is finished" means *"The debt has been paid in full!"*

God came! Jesus became the Passover for the world! It's no wonder John the Baptist introduced Jesus by saying, "Behold, the Lamb!" (John 1:29, NASB). It's no wonder Paul wrote, "Christ our Passover Lamb has been sacrificed" (1 Cor. 5:7). Passover is Jesus![2]

HIDING THE AFIKOMEN

Even today, the celebration of Passover is all about Jesus! At the beginning of many Jewish Passover celebrations, the father of the house performs an interesting ceremony. It's called "hiding the afikomen." (This part of the Passover ceremony is very old, probably dating back as far as the first century. I've never met anyone who knows what it means; it's just tradition. Yet it is done in millions of Jewish households all over the world every Passover night.)[3]

To perform the afikomen ceremony, the father of the house takes a cloth bag called an afikomen bag. It's also called a "unity bag." In that unity bag are three pockets. Before the feast the father puts three sheets of unleavened bread (matzo) in the unity bag, one in each pocket. At the beginning of the meal the father takes the middle piece of matzo out of the bag. (This is the *middle piece of the three* matzos *in the unity.*)

This piece of matzo is called the afikomen. Amazingly, afikomen is not a Hebrew word—it's Greek! It comes from the

Greek word *aphikomenos*,[4] which can be translated "He who is coming!" or "the coming One!"

The Jewish people have strict rules about how matzo is prepared. It has to be pierced, striped, and bruised. If you hold a piece of unleavened bread up to the light, you will see light coming through the holes pierced in the matzo. So the father picks up this bruised, striped, pierced afikomen—the middle one of the three in the unity—which is the piece of matzo representing "the coming One." And then he *breaks* it! After that he carefully wraps it in a white linen napkin and hides it until later in the Passover meal.

At the close of the meal, the children are told to search for the afikomen, and the one who finds it gets a reward. When the afikomen is found, it is unwrapped and held up for all to see. Now, think about this; picture it in your mind: When the afikomen was broken, it symbolized Jesus' death. When it was wrapped in linen, it represented the wrapping of His body in linen after His death.

When the wrapped afikomen is hidden from sight, it symbolizes His burial. Finally, it is unwrapped and held up for all to see. This symbolizes the *resurrection* of Jesus!

That's the whole gospel story in the middle of a Jewish Passover celebration! When the afikomen is found, it is then eaten. (Usually each person gets a piece.) This is the point in the last supper when Jesus lifted the bread and said, "This is my body, given for you." (See Luke 22:19.) Jesus was saying, "I am the afikomen. I am the coming One." He was identifying Himself with the Passover celebration!

After the afikomen is eaten, a cup of wine is poured. The Jewish people call it "the cup of redemption." This is the point in the last supper when Jesus lifted the cup and said, "This cup is the new covenant in my blood; do this, whenever you drink it, in remembrance of me" (1 Cor. 11:25, NIV). This was the original context of the Lord's Supper! The Lord's Supper was given in the context of a Passover meal. When Jesus said, "I have eagerly desired to eat this meal with you," He was talking about the Passover meal. (See Luke 22:15.) I believe He still desires to share Passover with His people!

PREPARING FOR PASSOVER

In studying how Passover is observed, it's interesting that there was a special time of *preparation* for Passover. As noted previously, before Passover could be celebrated, the people were to cleanse their homes from impurity. This is still done today in observant Jewish households. Jewish families diligently search their homes, looking on every shelf, in every drawer, and in every cabinet to find any trace of leaven. (Leaven is often used to symbolize sin and impurity.) If any leaven (impurity) is discovered, it is removed before the Passover celebration begins.[5]

This is good for us to do today. Before experiencing God's deliverance, it's important to search your home and remove impurity. To help you do this, I've written a book with Rebecca Wagner Sytsema called *Protecting Your Home from Spiritual Darkness*, which describes how to go through your home and remove defilement and impurity. We have received many, many testimonies of how ridding a home of spiritual darkness has broken demonic oppression and released the blessing of God over the home. God wanted this *breaking of demonic oppression* to be a yearly part of His cycle of life—thus, Passover!

Here are some suggestions for preparing your home for Passover:

1. Dedicate your home to the Lord. Pray and invite the presence of God into your home. Ask the Lord to use your home for His purposes.

2. Take a spiritual inventory of your home. Ask God to give you discernment as you look at what you own. Go through your house, room by room, and let the Holy Spirit show you any objects that should not be in your home. Particularly note the following:

   • Objects depicting false gods

   • Objects used in pagan worship, occult practices, or witchcraft

   • Objects exalting or promoting evil

   • Objects related to past sin

   • Objects that have become idols in your life

3. Cleanse your home of ungodly objects. Deuteronomy 7:25 says such objects should be destroyed by fire. Take what can be burned and burn it in an appropriate place. If it cannot be burned, pass it through the fire (as a symbolic act of obedience) and then destroy it by whatever means is appropriate, such as smashing or flushing.

   Note: If you have a roommate or spouse, do not remove items belonging to him or her without permission!

4. Ask forgiveness. Once you have destroyed the object, renounce any participation you or your family have had with that object, and ask God to forgive you.

5. Cleanse each room and cleanse the land. Go through your house and repent for any known sin that has been committed in each room. Pray that the Lord would heal any trauma caused by the torment of

demonic forces in your home. Pray over your property as well.

6. Consecrate your home and property to God and His service. Declare Joshua 24:15 over your home, "As for me and my household, we will serve the Lord" (NIV)!

7. Fill your home with glory. Take Communion at home as a family. Sing praises and pray in your home. Testify about the good things God has done for you. Speak the Word in your house. Read the Psalms aloud. Play praise music. Keep your house bright. Cultivate a mood of hope in your home. Refuse any influence that would extinguish the brightness of God's glory.

When you have removed all spiritual defilement, speak a blessing over your house and invite the presence of God to fill it!

Notes

CHAPTER 1

1. "Covid-19," New Scientist, updated April 14, 2020, https://www.newscientist.com/term/covid-19/#ixzz6IMyD23KU.

2. "What You Need to Know About Coronavirus," *Washington Post*, April 6, 2020, https://www.washingtonpost.com/health/2020/02/28/what-you-need-know-about-coronavirus/?arc404=true.

3. "What You Need to Know About Coronavirus," *Washington Post*; Stephanie M. Lee, "'Silent Carriers' Are Helping Spread the Coronavirus. Here's What We Know About Them," BuzzFeed, April 2, 2020, https://www.buzzfeednews.com/article/stephaniemlee/coronavirus-asymptomatic-silent-carrier-spread-contagious.

4. Damian Eisner, "Pesach Miracles: A Purpose Beyond Belief," First Fruits of Zion, March 30, 2020, https://ffoz.org/discover/passover/pesach-miracles-a-purpose-beyond-belief.html.

5. Richard Elliott Friedman, *Commentary on the Torah* (New York: HarperOne, 2001), 218, as quoted in Eisner, "Pesach Miracles."

6. Eisner, "Pesach Miracles."

CHAPTER 2

1. Chuck D. Pierce, *God's Unfolding Battle Plan* (Bloomington, MN: Chosen Books, 2007), 81.

2. Worldometer, accessed May 10, 2020, www.worldometers.info.

3. Brian Resnick and Christina Animashaun, "Why Covid-19 Is Worse Than the Flu, in One Chart," Vox, March 18, 2020, https://www.vox.com/science-and-health/2020/3/18/21184992/coronavirus-covid-19-flu-comparison-chart?.

4. Chuck D. Pierce and Robert Heidler, *A Time to Prosper* (Bloomington, MN: Chosen Books, 2013), 99–100.

5. Portions of this chapter are taken from Chuck D. Pierce, *Time to Defeat the Devil* (Lake Mary, FL: Charisma House, 2011), 63–80.

Plague five is quoted from Chuck D. Pierce and Rebecca Wagner Sytsema, *The Future War of the Church* (Ventura, CA: Regal Books, 2007), 155.

6. Pierce and Heidler, *A Time to Prosper*, 108–9.

7. Aaron Schnoor, "Is the Coronavirus the New Black Plague? An Examination of 2,500 Years of Epidemics," Lessons From History, March 5, 2020, https://medium.com/lessons-from-history/is-the-coronavirus-the-new-black-plague-31f93d2bbfd6.

CHAPTER 3

1. "Francis of Assisi Quotes," BrainyQuote, accessed May 6, 2020, https://www.brainyquote.com/quotes/francis_of_assisi_121023.

2. Chuck D. Pierce and Rebecca Wagner Sytsema, *The Spiritual Warfare Handbook* (Bloomington, MN: Chosen Books, 2016), 27–28, https://books.google.com/books?id=5OstCwAAQBAJ&q.

3. Pierce and Sytsema, *The Spiritual Warfare Handbook*, 28.

4. Pierce and Sytsema, *The Spiritual Warfare Handbook*, 28–29.

5. *The Future War of the Church*, *God's Unfolding Battle Plan*, and *A Time to Triumph*.

CHAPTER 4

1. Chuck D. Pierce and Robert Heidler, *Restoring Your Shield of Faith* (Bloomington, MN: Chosen Books, 2004), 139.

2. Anne Tate, personal communication, March 30, 2020.

3. Tate, personal communication.

4. Adam Taggart, "Economic Shockwaves," PeakProsperity.com, March 31, 2020, https://www.peakprosperity.com/economic-shockwaves/.

5. Blue Letter Bible, s.v. "*paqad*," accessed May 6, 2020, https://www.blueletterbible.org/lang/Lexicon/Lexicon.cfm?strongs=H6485&t=KJV.

6. Adrian R. Bell, Andrew Prescott, and Helen Lacey, "The Coronavirus Is NOT the Black Plague (But It Can Teach Us Lessons)," *National Interest*, March 4, 2020, https://nationalinterest.org/blog/buzz/coronavirus-not-black-plague-it-can-teach-us-lessons-129607.

7. Pierce, *God's Unfolding Battle Plan*, 169.

8. "Newton's Law of Universal Gravitation," formulated in Newton's *Philosophiae Naturalis Principia Mathematica*, first published in 1687.

9. Pierce and Heidler, *A Time to Prosper*, 214–15.

10. Adapted from Pierce and Heidler, *A Time to Prosper*, 213–14.

CHAPTER 5

1. Mark Landler, "Trump Recognizes Jerusalem as Israel's Capital and Orders U.S. Embassy to Move," *New York Times*, December 6, 2017, https://www.nytimes.com/2017/12/06/world/middleeast/trump-jerusalem-israel-capital.html.

2. Justin Rana, personal communication, March 31, 2020.

3. Daniel and Amber Pierce, *Joy in the War*, chapter 7.

4. Pierce, *Joy in the War*, chapter 7

5. Pierce, *Joy in the War*, chapter 7.

6. Linda Heidler, personal communication, April 1, 2020.

CHAPTER 6

1. Candice Hunter Kennedy, "It is not going good," Facebook, March 19, 2020, https://www.facebook.com/candice.hunterkennedy/posts/10157384653864514.

2. Robert Heidler, personal communication, April 1, 2020.

3. R. Heidler, personal communication.

4. Procopius, *Secret History,* trans. Richard Atwater (Ann Arbor, MI: University of Michigan Press, 1961), https://sourcebooks.fordham.edu/basis/procop-anec.asp.

5. Procopius, *Secret History.*

6. David Keys, *Catastrophe: An Investigation Into the Origins of the Modern World* (New York: Ballantine, 2000), https://books.google.com/books?id=wpGN4ekwHgYC.

7. Keys, *Catastrophe.*

8. J. A. S. Evans, *The Age of Justinian: The Circumstances of Imperial Power* (New York: Routledge, 2001), 164, https://books.google.com/books?id=jjSDAgAAQBAJ.

9. See also Robert D. Heidler, *The Messianic Church Arising!* (Denton, TX: Glory of Zion International Ministries Inc., 2006).

CHAPTER 7

1. Rich Lowry, "Blaming the WHO and China Is Not Scapegoating," *Politico*, April 8, 2020, https://www.politico.com/news/magazine/2020/04/08/who-china-trump-coronavirus-176242?cid=apn.
2. Eleanor Albert, "Christianity in China," Council on Foreign Relations, updated October 11, 2018, https://www.cfr.org/backgrounder/christianity-china.
3. Lisa Lyons, personal communication, March 31, 2020.
4. Chuck D. Pierce and Robert Heidler, *A Triumphant Kingdom* (Denton, TX: Glory of Zion International Ministries, 2019).

APPENDIX

1. Much of the section comparing the events of the Passover with Jesus' crucifixion is adapted from Pierce, *Time to Defeat the Devil*, 83–84.
2. Pierce and Heidler, *A Time to Prosper*, 110–11.
3. Teaching on the afikomen is adapted from Pierce and Heidler, *A Time to Prosper*, 111–13.
4. Peter G. Bolt, *The Cross from a Distance* (Downers Grove, IL: InterVarsity Press, 2004), 104.
5. Section on preparing for Passover is adapted from Pierce and Heidler, *A Time to Prosper*, 114–15.